Praise for
What Went Wrong at

"Do not put another dime into the stock market before reading this book. In all the millions of words that have been written about the Enron scandal, these are the first that really explain, in a way anyone can understand, what actually happened in the greatest stock swindle of modern times. You'll learn what Enron's business really consisted of, how the accounting for it really worked, and who the key executives really were . . . in particular chairman Kenneth Lay, the proselytizing son of a Missouri preacher, and Lay's protégé, Jeffrey Skilling, who earned the nickname of Darth Vader for his ruthless behavior. You'll follow Enron's forays into everything from the Internet to the California energy market, learning how Skilling and Lay influenced Wall Street analysts to say only favorable things about the company, and what happened to the analysts who didn't oblige. And you'll behold the inevitable doom that eventually comes to shareholders who believe that rising stock prices are proof of increasing value. In the end they may be proof of nothing more than what the world has now come to know as 'Enronitis.' This is the book that explains what that word really means."

—Christopher Byron, author, *Martha Inc.*

"The Enron story, for most of us, is a monster. Fusaro and Miller clarify what went wrong in a manner that allows anyone to get their arms around the beast quickly, without killing oneself."

—Bill Crawford, former *Chicago Tribune* financial writer and Pulitzer Prize winner

"The authors' sharp insights into Enron's self-destructive culture provide a clear road map into its massive failure."

—Peter Behr, *Washington Post* financial writer

WHAT WENT WRONG AT ENRON

Everyone's Guide to the Largest Bankruptcy in U.S. History

PETER C. FUSARO
ROSS M. MILLER

JOHN WILEY & SONS, INC.

Published by John Wiley & Sons, Inc., Hoboken, New Jersey
Published simultaneously in Canada

For general information on our other products and services, or technical support, please contact our Customer Care Department within the United States at 800-762-2974, outside the United States at 317-572-3993 or fax 317-572-4002.

Wiley also publishes its books in a variety of electronic formats. Some content that appears in print may not be available in electronic books.

ISBN 0-471-26574-8

Printed in the United States of America.

10 9 8 7 6 5 4 3 2 1

Contents

Preface: In the Beginning . . .

In the summer of 1977, typical American preteens found themselves caught in the grips of a mania that was sweeping the country. *Star Wars*, an epic science-fiction saga of life "a long time ago in a galaxy far, far away" was playing at theaters everywhere, with some children lining up to see the George Lucas film time and time again.

Star Wars was also a merchandizing phenomenon. Action figures, light sabers, and assorted paraphernalia were sold for the multitude of fans to relive their screen fantasies at home. One of the early successes from among the vast array of *Star Wars* collectibles was the *Star Wars* trading cards issued by Topps, the company behind an earlier boom in baseball cards. While Topps had created small collections of trading cards for other media creations before, *Star Wars* cards were so popular that in the first year it released five separate series of the cards. The complete set of 330 cards (and 55 accompanying stickers) was sufficiently large to make securing an entire collection through the purchase of individual packs of cards almost as difficult as it was for the even larger sets of baseball cards.

The preteen boys (and a growing number of girls thanks in large part to the brave and feisty Princess Leia) who were the target market for the cards quickly learned that obtaining a complete set of even one of the five series of cards was not a solo effort. Even if Topps, like other issuers of collectible cards, had not cleverly stacked the deck to make it difficult to acquire a complete collection, the basic laws of probability indicate that it is necessary for an individual to purchase thousands of cards in order to complete the collection of 330. By trading duplicate or less desirable cards with other children, a complete collection could be obtained more quickly and less expensively.

It seems that in every neighborhood there is one card trader extraordinaire—the kid who makes the cards his mission in life. He learns which cards are hot and which cards are not and tends to be on the best side of every deal. He cleverly comes up with deals that no one else could even imagine. If someone has a card he desperately needs but he does not have anything to trade for it, this trading whiz will make a deal by promising certain of the cards he gets when they go the store later that day to buy cards.

Just as some of the trading card whizzes of the 1960s found themselves in Wall Street trading rooms during the financial boom of the 1980s, an expert at trading *Star Wars* cards was equally as likely to turn up at Enron in the 1990s. Just about any deal that one can devise using trading cards has its counterpart with stocks, bonds, options, natural gas, electricity, and even bandwidth (data transmission over fiber-optic cables). Some of the language is even the same; one of the most common types of trades is known simply as a swap.

Of course, just about the time that *Star Wars* cards were a fad, leaps in information technology coupled with financial deregulation coalesced into a boom that lifted the economy out of the stagflation of the 1970s and into the longest economic expansion in history and a bonanza for traders and deal makers. Enron not only jumped on that wave, but helped create it.

How? The *Star Wars* movie itself was a prime example of how business used the financial system to help it move on to bigger (and arguably better) things. Like Steven Spielberg's pioneering blockbuster *Jaws*, which enticed moviegoers two summers earlier, *Star Wars* not only cost a fortune to make, but the budgets for distributing and promoting the film were huge as well. Movie studios found themselves in the position of the kid who wants a trading card but would have to trade something for it until he gets his allowance. (For the moviemakers, their allowance was the share of ticket receipts from the theater box offices once the movie was released.) As it spent more money to make bigger movies, Hollywood had less money to get copies of the films into theaters and to entice people to see them through advertising and other promotional efforts. The theaters could not kick in much, as they seemed always to be flirting with financial disaster themselves.

Fortunately for Hollywood and the movie-viewing public, Wall Street deal makers came to the rescue. In the 1990s, a variety of special purpose entities (SPEs) were developed to finance the distribution of movies. Rather than burden either the moviemakers or the theaters with the debt required to get a movie shown, these SPEs were separate companies whose only purpose was to borrow money for a few months to get films into theaters. Most of the early box office receipts for the movie would go directly to the SPE to pay off the loan. In order to insure against any one film being a bomb and preventing repayment, several films were bundled together into each SPE and other measures were taken to make it a virtual certainty that the loan would be paid off completely. Indeed, the short-term debt issued by this type of SPE is considered safe enough by ratings agencies that many money market mutual funds can purchase it for their investors without fear of loss. Much of this safety comes from the fact that the films themselves serve as collateral. Furthermore, because these SPEs are designed to be "bankruptcy remote," payment is assured even if the movie studio or the theaters go bankrupt.

Getting back to trading cards, it is important to realize that not all trades are fair. The younger members of the neighborhood are easy prey, especially in the absence of parental supervision. Furthermore, innocent card trading can easily degenerate into gambling where the winner is determined by how the cards are flipped or tossed. Finally, as the stakes grow larger, the temptation to cheat and steal increases. While most children are honest by nature, the attraction of a quick and easy gain is enough to lure some of them over to the dark side.

The story of Enron is the story of how a group of people, who could well have traded *Star Wars* or some other kind of trading cards as children, went bad and took the fortunes of a large company, its employees, and its investors with them. Enron began its life in 1985 as a sleepy Houston utility that dealt almost exclusively in natural gas. It quickly went on to trade almost anything that could be traded, constructing a trading room in Houston so flashy that it put the deck of the *Millennium Falcon* to shame. As it grew, Enron traders prospered and could soon afford toys that exceeded their wildest childhood dreams.

As we shall see, no single misstep brought Enron to the brink. A series of missteps (both accidental and calculated) and just plain bad luck brought Enron's more nefarious dealings to light, precipitating its ultimate collapse. The dirtiest of Enron's deals involved SPEs of its own construction that sported names straight from *Star Wars* such as Chewco (from Chewbacca the Wookie). While Enron's traders may still have inhabited the fantasy worlds of their youth, their trades had a harsh reality to them that touched the heart and soul of American life. Who got electricity during California's energy crisis, which farms would have water to irrigate their crops, and other decisions that were critical to the smooth operation of the largest economy in the world were being made in Enron's trading rooms. Aided by their accountants at Arthur Andersen, some of whom then moved on to cushy jobs at Enron, the "Star Wars" SPEs were not the innocent financing vehicles used by Hollywood and the rest of the corporate world, but helped cook Enron's books and funnel vast sums of money to its key financial officers. Darth Vader would certainly have been proud of Enron.

Enron's bankruptcy was devastating to those who worked there. While those at the top of the company were responsible for its collapse, they had sold enough of their stock to bank away tens and in some cases hundreds of millions of dollars. The decent people who worked under them would lose not only their jobs, but in many cases their life savings including the funds in their 401(k) plans that they had invested in Enron stock. Their stock purchases were encouraged by the same executives who were selling their own stock.

Enron's misery would spread well beyond the company itself. The salaries of Enron's workers had helped make the city of Houston prosperous and vibrant—restaurants, stores, and other merchants would suffer from the loss of their business. Many public and private pension funds had invested heavily in Enron, a company that until the very end would be rated "buy" or "strong buy" by almost every brokerage that covered it, with many placing it on their recommended list of top stock picks.

That Enron, a company admirable for its innovations, could fall so far so fast undermined confidence in other U.S. stocks. Investors were concerned that if they could not trust Enron, then what company could they trust? Even more disturbing to some was the impression that Enron had tried to co-opt the political establishment through massive and wide-ranging campaign contributions. Enron's chairman, Kenneth Lay, was not only on good terms with George W. Bush, he was a strong supporter of Al Gore's environmental program. It seemed that Enron would get in bed with any politician who could wield influence on its behalf.

While Enron may well be the most spectacular and scandalous business failure in history, at its core was a good idea that will live on long after memory of it fades away. In an increasingly networked world, companies that make it easy for people and businesses to trade—that set fair rules of engagement and honor those rules themselves—will likely prosper. Indeed, a notable rare success to come out of the Internet boom is eBay, an auction company that in many ways was the polar opposite of Enron in terms of how stuff could be traded electronically. Even though 25 years have passed since *Star Wars* trading cards were first issued, those who still have an itch to trade them will find an active market on eBay. In light of the disasters that have befallen Enron and most other Internet-related ventures, *Star Wars* cards have made rather nice investments, with any one of them trading for substantially more than a share of Enron stock.

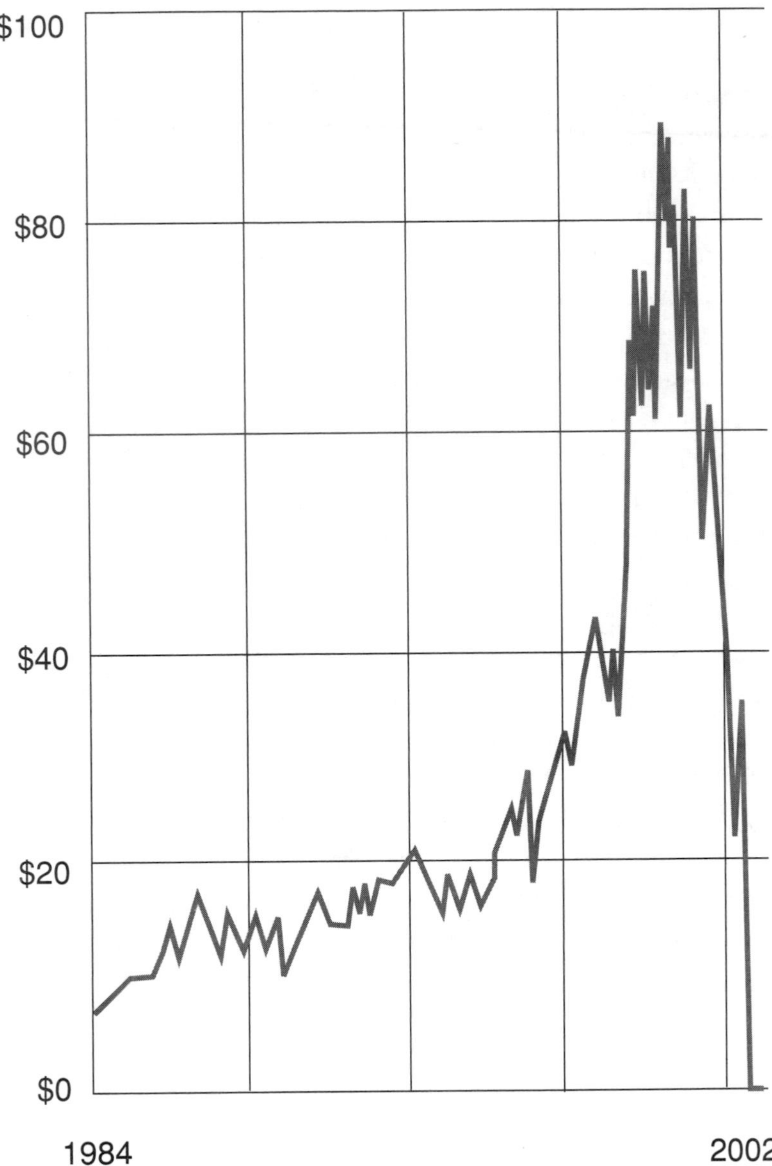

Enron Stock Price

Data Source: New York Stock Exchange, Nasdaq OTC.

WHAT WENT WRONG AT ENRON

1

Ken Lay's Junk Bond Ride Up on the Natural Gas Express

A popular notion as to why Enron failed is that its leaders didn't "stick to their knitting." When Ken Lay joined Houston Natural Gas (the firm that would grow to become Enron) as its chief executive officer (CEO) in 1984, the company was an undistinguished utility whose business focused on moving natural gas through the pipelines that were its major assets, extending thousands of miles across the United States. Over time, Enron became a trading giant that would play a major role in every new market that came along, luring away some of Wall Street's top talent in the process. But in the late 1980s and early 1990s, the deregulating natural gas and electricity markets would be its bread and butter both as an energy company and as a Wall Street type trading firm. While there can be no question that Enron's hubris caused it to eventually overextend itself, entering markets where it had no business being, its initial inclination to expand was a sound business decision.

From the beginning, Enron was different from other companies. Most successful companies trace their roots to a powerful innovator and the products that grew out of his or her innovation. Thomas Edison's lightbulb ultimately became the General Electric Company. Bill Gates's brilliant marketing of a personal computer operating system laid the foundation for Microsoft. In contrast, Enron was based on an idea. While Ken Lay, Enron's founder, did not think of the idea that fueled Enron's growth, he embraced and advocated it with the fervor that one might expect from the son of a Baptist minister from rural Missouri. The idea that drove Ken Lay and fueled Enron was that of the power of the free market system.

Ken Lay's background was quite unlike that of a typical corporate chieftain, most of whom have formal training in engineering and/or management. All of Ken Lay's degrees, including his Ph.D. from the University of Houston, were in economics. Among the many positions he held before he settled down at Enron was a job teaching economics as an assistant professor at George Washington University. Ken Lay could easily have ended up writing policy papers at a conservative think tank or as a pundit on a cable news network, but instead he became head of one of the largest (and for a time one of the most respected) companies in the United States.

In the 1980s, the world's image of Texas businessmen was shaped by the television show *Dallas*, which centered on the chicanery of Texas oil baron J. R. Ewing. The fictional J. R., played to perfection by Larry Hagman, epitomized what many people saw to be the evils of the market system. He sold a dirty product, crude oil, and employed even dirtier means to get his way. J. R. Ewing's behavior went far beyond that of a typical capitalist to that of an out-and-out anarchist. To him, the rules of the market were meant to be broken whenever it was convenient. In contrast, Ken Lay dealt in a relatively clean product, natural gas.

Until demand for energy started to outstrip supply in the 1960s, oilmen found natural gas to be a nuisance. Crude oil and natural gas were often discovered together, and oilmen would have to burn the gas off in large flares in order to extract the oil. Fortunately for the blue skies of Texas, natural gas, unlike oil and other fossil fuels, burns very cleanly. Still, the growth in the big cities of Texas and California, as well as other sprawling metropolitan areas that relied on the automobile for transportation, led to a growing pollution problem that by the 1960s could no longer be ignored. With other alternative energy sources still on the drawing board, environmentalists embraced natural gas as the only fossil fuel to provide a clean alternative to petroleum products.

HOUSTON'S J. R. OF NATURAL GAS

Before we explore where Ken Lay's crusade for natural gas ultimately led him, it is worth noting that Ken Lay and J. R.

Ewing did have many things in common. Lay was not known for tolerating rivals, even if they had been close business associates for some time. At Enron, for example, the vice chairman's position was known by many Enron senior executives as the "ejector seat." Those who had been ejected from this number two position, or jumped out themselves, included executives such as Richard Kinder, Rebecca Mark, Cliff Baxter, and Joseph Sutton, all of whom held the vice chairman's role in title or function. It seemed that the faster Enron grew, the sooner it would need a new vice chairman. Furthermore, like J. R., Ken Lay exerted political influence and deal-making savvy to have the rules changed in ways that worked in his and Enron's favor. Lay's transformation of Houston National Gas into Enron, and his ability to remain in the driver's seat, would certainly have earned one of J. R. Ewing's trademark grins.

When Lay took the reins of Houston Natural Gas in 1984, he faced an enormous problem. Houston Natural Gas was a relatively small company, and Wall Street was in the midst of a mergers and acquisitions binge in which the little fish were becoming an endangered species with so many big fish eager to swallow them up. Indeed, Kenneth Lay came to the attention of the board of directors of Houston Natural Gas when the company was in the process of fending off a hostile takeover bid from Coastal Corp. He was quickly able to double the size of the company by acquiring two other natural-gas companies, Florida Gas and Transwestern Pipeline. Lay's next move was to team up with InterNorth, a similar company based in Omaha, Nebraska, whose pipelines were a natural fit with Lay's. Though InterNorth saw itself as acquiring Houston Natural Gas, Lay pitched it to his people as a merger. Sure enough, it took only a year for him to wrest control of the new company, which was now called Enron, from its CEO, Samuel Segnar. By itself, the new name was a signal of the company's ambition, given its resemblance to that of Exxon, the energy giant where Ken Lay had started his career in 1965 when the Houston division was known as Humble Oil.

In the process of creating Enron, Ken Lay had to fight off a bid by Irwin Jacobs, the renowned corporate raider, to take over the company. Jacobs had accumulated a substantial stake in InterNorth before the merger, and Enron got rid of him by buying back this stake at a substantial premium. Jacobs' tactic of mounting a threat to take over a company for the purpose of selling the shares back to it at a huge profit, something Gordon Gekko did in the 1987 movie *Wall Street*, was popularly known as "greenmail."

Ken Lay could only save Enron from the clutches of Irwin Jacobs by using $230 million in excess funds in the employee pension fund to buy stock and by borrowing the money to pay him off. To get this money, Ken enlisted the aid of Michael Milken, Wall Street's junk bond king who operated out of the Beverly Hills branch of Drexel Burnham Lambert. Until Milken came along, Drexel was a second-rate New York investment bank. It then quickly gained prominence as the premier issuer of junk bonds before collapsing in 1990 as the result of a scandal that would ultimately send Michael Milken to prison.

Like Ken Lay, Michael Milken was an idea man. His big idea came from research that he conducted as a student at the Wharton School of Finance. He found that corporate bonds that the ratings agencies did not consider worthy of gaining their seal of approval in the form of an investment-grade rating, which came to be known as junk bonds, were a great investment. Financial markets tended to avoid such bonds, so their prices were usually much lower than their true value. If Milken's reasoning had stopped there, that insight alone could have made him quite wealthy, but he took things another step further and became filthy rich as a result.

The bonds that Milken studied were mostly "fallen angels." These bonds were investment grade when they were issued but over time had fallen out of favor with the agencies (led by Standard & Poor's and Moody's Investors Service) that rate them. Usually these downgrades were the result of business setbacks that drained a company's financial resources and raised the possibility that it might eventually default on its bond payments. The main reason that the price of a bond that fell into disgrace could plunge to bargain levels was that large investment managers, especially those who managed pension funds, were legally bound to hold only investment-grade bonds. In general, the companies that had the financial strength to issue bonds were large companies, leaving smaller companies out of the financial markets and at the mercy of banks.

Michael Milken, though sheer force of will and hard work, created a new financial market in which smaller companies could issue junk bonds and investors could buy them, making both sides better off and generating huge fees for Milken and his Drexel Burnham brethren that had no precedent on Wall Street. Milken not only helped companies to issue junk bonds, he increased their value to investors by maintaining an active secondary market for them after they were issued. (Unlike stocks, only a tiny fraction of all bonds are traded on public exchanges.) The main problem with junk-bond financing is that investment bankers, lacking the regulatory oversight of their less well compensated counterparts at commercial banks, in the heat of competition could make one bad deal after another. Such deals would overload the issuing company with debt to the point where one wrong move could drive it into bankruptcy. The investors in the junk bonds would suffer as well because the value of their investment would be reduced to whatever they could salvage in bankruptcy court, which often was pennies on the dollar. In the short run, the deal makers would profit from their huge fees, but as bankruptcies increased, which they did in the early 1990s, they would become the lepers of Wall Street for several years.

As the money that could be made from junk bonds increased, so did the tendency to violate securities laws. The biggest offender was Ivan Boesky, whose "greed is good" attitude and insider-trading activity inspired the creation of the Gordon Gekko character in *Wall Street.* Milken had close ties to Boesky, and those ties ultimately got Milken a prison sentence as part of a plea bargain. While Milken maintains his innocence, his poor judgment in picking his business partners in the process of building his empire led to his downfall regardless of whether he truly committed a crime.

A MOUNTAIN OF DEBT

Ken Lay, who kept in contact with Michael Milken years after Milken was released from prison, clearly viewed him as a kind of role model. Making a new market, as Milken did with junk bonds, could be the road to fantastic wealth. Unfortunately, Ken Lay failed to heed the lessons of Milken's failure. He often rubbed elbows with this controversial figure in finance, including a private meeting in May 2001 that was purportedly held to drum up support for Lay's solution to California's energy crisis. To say the least, Milken was a strange but visible guest to this secretive meeting, which included luminaries such as Arnold Schwarzenegger and Richard Riordan, the mayor of Los Angeles. These were lessons that Lay would end up experiencing for himself in his own way.

With control of Enron secured by a mountain of debt obtained with Milken's assistance, Ken Lay faced an enormous challenge to Enron's future. He believed fervently in free markets, but the market for natural gas was about as far from free as you could find in the United States.

The problem began with the Arab oil embargo in 1973, when the Nixon administration imposed wage and price controls in a failed effort to keep inflation manageable. Most wage and price controls were removed as their futility became apparent and were replaced by such laughable efforts as the WIN (Whip Inflation Now) button campaign of the Ford administration. Energy prices, however, remained under federal control.

Like Forrest Gump, who magically appeared in the

background at critical points in history, Ken Lay left Houston for a while during the early 1970s to work in the federal energy bureaucracy and rose to the position of deputy undersecretary of energy at the Interior Department. As one of the few avid proponents of free markets at the time, he attracted some attention by his arguments for the deregulation of natural gas. It would be nearly a decade before serious efforts at deregulating the industry would make it into law.

ENRON RIDES DEREGULATION WAVE

As Enron was being born in 1985, the Reagan administration was in the process of dismantling the price regulation that had inhibited the growth of the natural gas industry. While both the Reagan and Bush administrations strongly backed deregulation, the enabling legislation would have to go through a Congress controlled by Democrats. Although it took several bills and lots of lobbying, by the time Bill Clinton took office in 1993 deregulation of natural gas at the federal level had run its course. What regulation remained was largely at the state level.

In the process of freeing Enron from the shackles of federal regulation, Ken Lay came to master another of J. R. Ewing's specialties—political hobnobbing. Indeed, as Enron grew, the charming Mr. Lay became its "outside man," leaving the day-to-day internal operation of the company to his underlings. Lay combined considerable charm, homespun roots, and economic expertise in a way that made him a natural to make the case for policies that would benefit Enron.

Lay and others at Enron contributed lavish amounts to politicians and the "soft money" institutions that helped fund them. He was a constant presence not only in both Bush administrations, but in the intervening Clinton administration as well. Because natural gas was seen as friendly to the environment, Lay was embraced by failed presidential candidate Al Gore, who supported the Kyoto Accords that his opponent George W. Bush and many other Republicans found unacceptable. Lay played both sides of the aisle so completely that when the matter of Enron came up for Congressional hearings in 2002, there were few key committee members who had not received campaign money from Enron.

Kenneth Lay's mastery of politics both inside his company in Houston and with the federal government in Washington was not enough to make the business successful. Like other companies burdened with junk bond interest payments to make, Enron had to either grow quickly or die. Enron came into existence with a natural-gas pipeline system that already spanned much of the United States, so further growth in that area was limited. However, deregulation of energy markets was creating new markets, new opportunities, and new temptations.

2

A Pattern of Less than Full Disclosure

With Enron's birth in the mid-1980s, Ken Lay found himself in the position of a boy with several boxes of trading cards that he had acquired from a string of mergers and acquisitions. The most important cards now in his possession were the natural-gas pipelines that formed a network crisscrossing the United States. But that was not all he had. In addition, he had numerous assets that produced natural gas, most of them oil wells that also pumped crude. Enron's asset collection came with a price attached to it—the junk bonds that were used to finance it. These bonds not only required hefty interest payments be made on a regular basis (junk bonds typically pay interest twice a year), but they usually had to be paid off within 10 years. Ken Lay was immediately placed in the position of putting the pieces together in such a way that he could sell off the assets that he deemed unnecessary while getting the most value out of the those he retained.

Enron's basic strategy was to keep the pipelines, and, as money was needed, sell off the oil wells. Ken Lay set up a subsidiary of Enron known as Enron Oil & Gas (in Texas, oil always comes first) to deal with both the wells and the ongoing oil and natural gas exploration projects. Enron started selling shares on Enron Oil & Gas to the public in 1989, and within 10 years all of it was sold off. Unlike its parent company, Enron Oil & Gas, which is now called EOG Resources (New York Stock Exchange ticker: EOG), has so far avoided financial distress and scandal.

Large assets sales not only helped Enron pay off its junk bonds as they came due, they also added to Enron's apparent earnings growth. For accounting purposes, a hard asset like an oil well is kept on a company's books at the price it paid to acquire it. If the asset increases in value in a given year and the owner continues to hold it, neither the company's income statement nor its balance sheet will reflect this gain. In accountants' terms, the company's "book value" is unaffected by changes in the value of the hard assets, such as oil wells and real estate, that it holds. One rationale for this is that because these assets are both costly and difficult to value each time a company prepares its books, it makes sense to keep these assets on the books at their acquisition cost. Hence, all the gains (or losses) in the value of an asset finally appear on a company's income statement at the time that the asset is sold.

Accountants have a considerable degree of discretion as to whether any gains are considered a normal component of earnings or merely an extraordinary event that is unlikely to recur. A company with a large number of assets that are worth more than their book values could easily create the impression of steadily increasing earnings by cleverly timing its asset sales. It could not, however, do this forever, as it would eventually run out of assets.

MARK-TO-MARKET INS AND OUTS

The problem of how to value assets and when to recognize their gains and losses is a problem that has been plaguing the accounting profession in a major way since the inflationary times of the 1970s. Accountants are often torn between reporting conservative numbers and using more accurate numbers. The traditional practice—conservative accounting—was to recognize decreases in the value of an asset as they occurred and increases in value only when the asset was sold. While this practice will keep company's books from exaggerating the company's value, it leads to enormous inconsistencies from one type of business to another. The trend has been to abandon this conservatism in favor of making accounting numbers reflect economic reality as closely as possible. Companies that hold assets that can be easily valued are encouraged (and in some cases, required) to use "mark-to-market" accounting for these assets. In mark-to-market accounting, the value of each asset is reassessed on a regular basis and changes in value are reflected in both the company's balance sheet and its income statement (from which its reported earnings are derived).

Judges in divorce proceedings will employ mark-to-market accounting in dividing the marital assets. If one spouse gets possession of the car, the judge will look up its value on the used car market, say $10,000, and then credit that amount to the settlement. This allows the judge to determine a fair split without actually selling the assets to determine their market price.

As we shall see, while mark-to-market looks great in theory, in practice it can be easily abused. Some assets that are subject to mark-to-market accounting do not have unambiguous market prices, and considerable judgment must be exercised in coming up with a suitable price. (Even the "closing prices" of stocks on the New York Stock Exchange depend on the clearing prices set by the Exchange's specialists—contrary to popular belief that they come from the last trade of the day.) The accountants who audit financial statements are supposed to ensure the legitimacy of mark-to-market valuation. In the case of Enron, however, this oversight was clearly lacking and contributed to Enron's eventual collapse.

Even if oil wells can sometimes be difficult to value for accounting purposes until the time of their sale, their underlying economics are relatively simple. Each well occupies a specific fixed location where oil and natural gas are extracted from it. Although the future of each well may be uncertain, which adds to the difficulty of valuing it, operating the well is not.

The tricky part of the energy business comes in getting energy to the factory or home where it is used. In the case of natural gas, the Central Intelligence Agency (CIA)'s *World Factbook* shows the United States as having a network of over 200,000 miles of gas pipeline, which is nearly five times as long as the 42,000 miles of the interstate highway system. In such a vast and complex network, there are literally thousands of ways to transport gas across the country, depending on which path one takes. The ability to understand the complexities of such a network and then use that understanding to trade in the deregulated markets for transporting gas through the network could, in principle, create riches that would dwarf Michael Milken's junk bond wealth.

Beginning in the 1940s, the problem of finding the least expensive way to move products through a network was among the most important problems in economics. It was also a major national defense issue during the Cold War. After World War II most of the top American economists served stints at the RAND Corporation's offices that overlooked the Pacific Ocean in Santa Monica examining related problems. Knowing what makes a transportation network work well is the same knowledge that is required to know how to destroy it with the fewest bombs. Indeed, the only Nobel Prize in economics to be jointly awarded to a Russian (Leonid Kantorovich) and an American (Tjalling Koopmans) was for the mathematics needed to solve such problems. Mathematician John Nash, who like Koopmans and many other Nobel laureates worked for a time at RAND, used similar methods to derive his contributions to game theory that were featured in Sylvia Nasar's best-selling biography, *A Beautiful Mind*, and the Oscar-winning movie based on it.

At the time of Enron's birth, the Texas oil and gas industry was already far ahead of Wall Street in its use of computer technology. The precursors of the scientific workstations that would spread through trading rooms in the late 1980s were being used to map oil and gas deposits in the early part of that decade. The annual Offshore Technology Conference, reputed to be the largest trade show in America, had exhibits of every high-tech gadget available at any price. The conference was so large that it not only filled all of Houston's Astrodome, it spilled over into most of the adjoining Astrodomain. Even fictional Texas was enamored of technology—J. R. Ewing had a personal computer on his desk more than a decade before Jack Welch at GE would deign to touch one.

Texas may have been a big player when it came to high technology, but it was not even in the game of high finance. The world's leading financiers tended to cluster around international financial centers such as New York, London, Tokyo, Zurich, Hong Kong, Singapore, Chicago, and San Francisco. Not only did Houston lack any world-class financial institutions of its own, but with financial deregulation its business increasingly went to out-of-state banks, such as California's Bank of America and Wells Fargo Bank, that set up branch offices there. Enron, with economist Ken Lay at its helm, was the best hope that Texas had to break into the big leagues.

When scientific workstations finally arrived in Wall

Street at just about the time Enron was born, investment bankers and traders immediately put them to good use. Like Texas, Wall Street had its own "good ol' boys" days that ended around 1975 with the advent of financial deregulation. Without the federal government to keep commissions up and interest rates down, only the smartest and fastest could make it through the tough times that followed.

As the computer began to spring up on every desktop throughout Wall Street and around the financial world, a new approach to high finance emerged. This "slice-and-dice" approach made its first big splash in the market for home mortgages. Traditionally, mortgages had worked the way that they are depicted in the Frank Capra movie *It's a Wonderful Life*. Home buyers who needed a mortgage to get the home of their dreams went to their local bank (or savings and loan), where the money they received came from local depositors. Of course, if a particular bank has too many home buyers or not enough depositors, this arrangement will not work very effectively. The solution is to turn the mortgages themselves into registered financial securities (like bonds) so that investors from around the world are able to purchase them and finance the mortgages in the process. Because matching homeowners with investors on a one-to-one basis would be too cumbersome, dozens of mortgages would be bundled together to form a single security known as a mortgage pass-through security. Shares in such a bundle could then be sold to investors.

This bundling of mortgages into securities (known as "securitization") was by itself revolutionary, but then Wall

Street took things a big step further. The problem that any investor in mortgages faces is that the mortgage holders are usually given the option to pay the mortgage off early. The two most common reasons for them to do this is moving to another home or being able to refinance at a lower interest rate. To pension funds and many other large institutional investors, these prepayments can be a deal killer. That is because these funds time their investments so that their cash flows match their expected future obligations, such as the payment of pensions to retirees. Wall Street investment bankers, however, saw that by arranging the mortgage payments into a series of three of more "tranches," it could slice out a new security from the primary tranche that would eliminate virtually all of the prepayments, pushing them off to the other tranches.

While there were some notable fiascoes along the way, computer technology made it so that securitization and the slice-and-dice view of finance that swept Wall Street changed the financial world forever. Michael Milken and the old-fashioned deal makers were losing ground to a new breed of financial rocket scientists who could make vast sums of money simply by rearranging the pieces of the vast financial puzzle that Wall Street had created. The age of the hedge fund had arrived, and Enron was there not long after the moment of creation.

SLICE-AND-DICE INVESTING

Hedge funds took the slice-and-dice mentality from creating securities to investing in them. The idea behind hedge funds comes from the solution to a common problem with investing—it is possible to be correct in predicting the fortunes of a specific stock or commodity and still lose money. Such unfortunate effects occur, for example, when you purchase a good stock in a bad market. You might buy stock in a biotech company at $30 per share in hopes that it will rise on the news that the Food and Drug Administration (FDA) has approved one of its drugs. If during the time that you are waiting for the announcement unfavorable market conditions depress all biotech stocks by 25 percent, then even when the good news comes, it might only bring your stock back to $28 per share, generating a loss of $2 per share instead of a far larger gain.

The solution to this problem is to create a hedge against the overall decline in biotech stocks. The simplest, although not completely effective, way to achieve the desired effect is a common hedging strategy known as pairs trading. At the same time that you purchase shares in your biotech company, you simultaneously sell short shares in a similar company for which you do not expect to have favorable news during the holding period. (Selling short involves borrowing shares, something a broker can arrange, and then selling them with the obligation to buy them back later, hopefully at a lower price—thus pocketing the difference.) With this hedge, any money lost from an overall decline in biotech shares is offset by a gain from the shares that were sold short. Using computers and boundless human ingenuity, hedge funds are capable of creating highly complex trades using combinations of securities that can target a specific event or anomaly in the markets and generate an enormous profit if things go right (or a shocking loss if they don't).

By their very nature, hedge funds need to operate in a top-secret environment. Therefore, they must be organized in a manner that they escape oversight by the United States securities laws. The standard means for achieving this is to incorporate offshore (outside the United States on an island such as those in the Caymans or Bahamas) and limit participation to a small number of institutional and very wealthy investors. Hedge fund managers take a generous share of any profits (from 15 to 50 percent) and can limit their investors' ability to withdraw their funds. Despite their high fees and keeping investors in the dark as to what is done with their money, the top hedge funds can be very choosy about whose money they will agree to manage.

At a basic level, the process used to pick the best path to move natural gas from one side of the country to the other is no different from that used to construct a clever and profitable hedge. Each involves looking at the pieces available in the market and then putting them together in the way that creates the best opportunity profit with the least risk of an unexpected loss. Moreover, with either pipelines or securities, a sufficiently clever trader (with lots of computer power) can often find ways to get rid of the risk altogether, thereby guaranteeing a profit at the end of the day. Hence, the expertise necessary for Enron to succeed at managing its pipelines in a deregulated world made hedge-fund type trading a natural expansion path for the firm.

A LEARNING EXPERIENCE

Ken Lay clearly saw that trading would be Enron's one big thing; so in 1985 Enron started a trading business in Valhalla. This Valhalla was not the legendary Norse paradise, but rather one of several communities in the lush suburbs north of New York City that would later host some of the largest and most notorious hedge funds. But this trading operation, which became Enron Oil in 1987, did not hedge its bets or pull its punches. It made one large bet after another on the future price of oil and lost most of those bets. Like a hedge fund, however, it was veiled in secrecy, keeping its secrets not only from the outside world but also from its owners back in Houston.

To corporate headquarters in Houston, Enron Oil was a star performer, adding about $50 million to its bottom line. But that was according to the books that the trading operation's management wanted Enron to see. By maintaining two sets of accounting books and some bank accounts that it controlled, Enron Oil was keeping Houston in the dark about all the losses that it had piled up. Enron apparently provided nothing in the way of oversight for this operation and learned about the fraud that was being perpetrated only when federal authorities, including U.S. district attorney and future mayor of New York City Rudolph Giuliani, entered the picture. The head of Enron Oil would go to prison.

The true extent of Enron Oil's losses will likely never be known, as the records necessary to reconstruct its activities have been missing for years. The size of the loss reported by Enron in its filings with the SEC was $85 million, but certain sources argue the loss grew as high as $142 million to $190 million once all was said and done.

Ken Lay has been quick to dismiss the Enron Oil affair as a mere detour along the path to success; however, in retrospect there are people both inside and outside the company who see it as an early warning sign of the troubles that would plague Enron in the future. The fact that the business failed

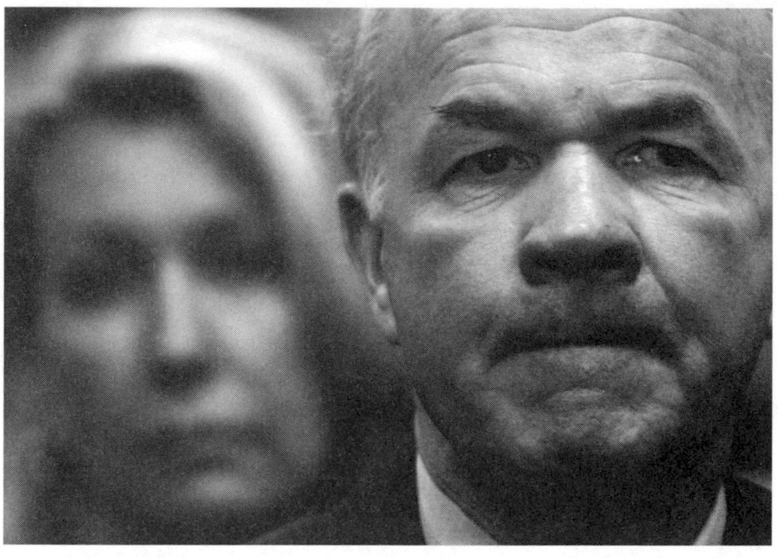

Former Enron Chairman and CEO Kenneth Lay refused to answer questions from lawmakers about his role in the collapse of the energy-trading giant for fear of incriminating himself during a hearing on Capitol Hill, February 12, 2002. (Reuters/Win McNamee, © Reuters NewMedia Inc./CORBIS)

because of managerial incompetence is not the real problem here; most entrepreneurial firms make a series of mistakes before they uncover the formula for success. What is disturbing is that Enron management turned a blind eye to activities that upon their discovery would shatter the illusion of rapidly growing earnings, and then apparently enlisted their accountants to cover up the true extent of the damage.

To Enron's credit, it clearly used the Enron Oil debacle as a learning experience. Going forward it would keep its trading operations close to home, over time creating a state-of-the-art facility at its Houston headquarters. It would also learn to do a better job of covering up its problems while creating a shiny facade for itself that would keep it above suspicion. The new team that Ken Lay brought into Enron in the wake of this early disaster would be more than up to the task.

3

The Skilling Case Study

Enron's initial efforts at building an energy trading operation in 1985 were hampered by a serious shortage of financial talent. Wall Street was in the middle of an unprecedented boom that would not be seen again until the heyday of the Internet in the late 1990s. Having exhausted the pool of applicants with the requisite technical backgrounds, Wall Street looked for anyone with brains who was willing to be retrained to do the Street's bidding. Top law school students by the dozen were lured to Wall Street firms not to do legal work but to be turned into traders and investment bankers. It is no wonder that in setting up its ill-fated Enron Oil operation the company had to entrust its fortune to strangers 1,500 miles away.

Everything changed after the October 1987 stock-market crash that saw the Dow Jones Industrial Average post its largest one-day percentage loss. Although the stock market rebounded from the crash and would go on to set new all-time highs within two years, the Wall Street jobs that were lost in the wake of the crash did not come back. Many investment banks fired massive numbers of their best-paid employees, and recruiting ground to a halt. Between 1989 and 1991 the excesses of the junk bond era came back to haunt the financial markets and, as company after company failed (including most savings and loan institutions), there were few new deals to be done.

Students leaving business schools who during the prior boom might have insisted on a job in New York or London would now consider going to Houston to work. Enron's window of opportunity for not only building a trading operation, but also crafting a world-class one in the process, had opened wide.

Ken Lay's most notable hire in the days that he was building up Enron came not from the new crop of business school graduates, but from the previous generation of students. In the 1970s, well before Wall Street set out on the longest boom in history, the top business school students could find their fortunes in management consulting. By systematically hoarding the best students graduating from business schools, often with the aid of professors who were either partners or close advisers, consulting firms could then rent this talent back to businesses at a premium price. These firms were natural magnets that attracted not only the brightest students, but, some would say, the most arrogant as well. Furthermore, companies often used the presence of top consultants to signal to the world that they were something special. It should come as no surprise then that Ken Lay would bring in consultants from one of the top consulting firms at the time, McKinsey & Company.

Of the stars from McKinsey who worked at Enron, Jeffrey Skilling would shine the brightest in Ken Lay's eyes. Lay hired him away from McKinsey to work at Enron (a standard career path for consultants) and groomed him to be his replacement. Despite an appearance before a Congressional committee early in 2002 where he seemed aware of little

Former Enron Chief Executive Officer Jeffrey Skilling testifies on Capitol Hill on February 26, 2002, before the Senate Commerce Committee hearing on Enron. Skilling told senators, "I didn't lie to Congress or anyone else" in denying he was aware of the company's precarious finances or its use of complex partnerships to hide debt. (AP Photo/Dennis Cook)

that went on at Enron during his short stint as CEO, Skilling must have had a remarkable memory and a rare ability to manage details in order to graduate near the top of his class as a Baker Scholar at Harvard Business School (HBS) and go on to make partner at McKinsey.

DAYS AT HARVARD

A story from Jeffrey Skilling's HBS student days may provide a telling glimpse into his character. HBS classes are typically conducted using the case method. Most cases are based on real business incidents, and students are presented with the problems that a business faced and must come up with solutions for themselves. Discussion of the cases, which helps determine a student's grade, is led by the professor in a pitlike classroom. A forgetful student unsure of the facts is quick to be ripped to shreds by other students looking to make their mark. In one such class, Jeffrey Skilling was asked what he would do if his company were producing a product that might cause harm—or even death—to the customers that used it. According to his professor at the time, former Congressman John LeBoutillier, Jeffrey Skilling replied: "I'd keep making and selling the product. My job as a businessman is to be a profit center and to maximize return to the shareholders. It's the government's job to step in if a product is dangerous." In an Enron culture seemingly obsessed with *Star Wars*, Skilling's bloodless demeanor led his colleagues to refer to him as "Darth Vader" behind his back.

Skilling's consulting assignment at Enron was beyond a

Harvard Business School case writer's wildest dreams. He had parachuted into Enron at a time when chaos reigned in the natural-gas industry. After years of cost-based government price regulation that guaranteed profits to everyone in the industry and effectively rewarded inefficiency and the failure to innovate, not only did companies have to compete for business, but prices, which had been relatively fixed, now fluctuated wildly. The problem was how to return the market to something like the artificial stability it had enjoyed before deregulation.

Jeff Skilling not only came up with the correct answer to this case but he also convinced Enron to break with the past and buy into the McKinsey vision of Enron's future. Deregulation freed up competition, but it did nothing to create the new markets that were required in order to reap the full benefits of competition. In particular, while it was no problem for industrial consumers of natural gas to purchase it on a day-to-day basis when the price was regulated (these purchases for immediate delivery are known as "spot" purchases), with prices fluctuating it became desirable to purchase gas ahead of time at a predetermined price for future delivery on a "forward" market.

In particular, both producers and consumers of natural gas were willing to enter into long-term forward contracts that fixed the price of natural gas rather than be at the mercy of the daily price fluctuations. Jeffrey Skilling and Enron need only look to Wall Street and the new financial markets that had been developed in the 1980s to find their blueprint. They determined that Wall Street's slice-and-dice financial technology was coming to Texas and Enron was to be the master chef.

The securitization of the U.S. market for home mortgages served as a useful starting point for what Enron was to do for the natural-gas market. Recall that in order to make home mortgages a suitable investment for pension funds and other institutional investors, investment banks bundled many home mortgages together and then carved out a prime cut (or tranche) that closely resembled an ordinary bond. This gave the big investors what they wanted—stable interest payments for years at a time—while allowing the individual homeowners to continue to prepay their mortgages whenever they desired. The only catch was that the investment bankers had to find someone to invest in the other tranches, which do not produce as reliable a flow of cash because the prepayments were apportioned to them. With proper butchering, investment bankers could create two or more additional tranches that investors with specific needs would find appetizing. Still, after all this carving, there were usually some pieces left over. These pieces came to be known as "toxic waste." These bits were not literally toxic; they were just so complex that it was difficult to assign a dollar value to them. Ideally, investment banks would structure deals so that it would not matter what the toxic waste was worth because the proceeds from the sale of the other tranches would more than cover the cost of the bundles of mortgages that had been sliced up.

Enron faced similar types of problems in creating a new market for natural gas. In the natural-gas market, consumers demand flexibility. (You may want to think of a typical consumer as an industrial company that requires natural gas for its production process or as a local utility that serves thousands of residential customers.) While the consumer would love to benefit from knowing what its gas will cost in advance, it does not want to be forced to purchase gas that it does not need or that is no longer economical to use. In other words, it is not as interested in buying the gas in advance as it is in having the *option* to buy it later at a fixed price. Likewise, producers might not wish to be committed to selling natural gas that they might have difficulty acquiring or that they might need for better-paying customers. They could then enter into a contract that gives them the option to sell the gas at a lower price than they might hope to receive, but high enough to cover their costs.

SKILLING'S GAS BANK

Jeffrey Skilling dealt with this problem by having Enron set up a "gas bank." The gas bank started out by arranging long-term contracts for natural gas with a group of suppliers. This is similar to an investment bank acquiring a pool of mortgages. It then took these contracts and determined the ways that it needed to slice and dice them to make them attractive to large natural-gas consumers. As noted, what consumers desired most were options. In addition, Enron provided price stability through the use of "swaps," which allowed one customer to swap a fixed price for a floating price, or vice versa, with Enron. Enron was happy to trade either side of the swap to earn its profits as the middleman. Enron made markets in both swaps and options, as well as more exotic deals that were little different from what a clever child might dream up when trading *Star Wars* cards.

Although energy swaps involved a bit more than the mere swapping of trading cards, the basic idea was the same and it also came from Wall Street. Even with its vast network of pipelines, Enron could not always deliver gas to its customers in a cost-effective manner. In these cases, it would design a swap contract that would not require it to deliver the natural gas itself. Instead, Enron would arrange to have a local distribution company deliver the natural gas to the consumer, and it would either pay or pocket any difference between what the gas cost and the price guaranteed in the contract. Enron swapped a fixed delivery price for the variable price available from the local distributor. Of course, Enron charged its customer a premium in exchange for the price stability it provided.

From the two basic building blocks of options and swaps, Enron was able to construct a vast array of contracts. For example, a simple combination of a swap and an option is known as a "swaption." Swaptions, like many of the other contracts that Enron offered, were not entirely its invention, but rather new versions of existing Wall Street products. Enron was a pioneer in creating standardized natural-gas contracts; the advantage of standardization was that these contracts were easy to understand and easy to trade. It also created a variety of custom contracts to meet the specific needs of natural-gas producers and consumers. The advantage of these contracts was that Enron could collect substantial fees for the effort that went into creating them.

As the middleman between producers and consumers, Enron was able to mark up prices because of the value that it added by giving each side what it wanted. However, just like an investment banker, Enron could be stuck holding pieces of gas contracts that exposed it to considerable risk. For example, it might be obligated to deliver gas to a consumer under conditions where prices were abnormally high due to an unexpected shortage. It was therefore critical for Enron to copy another page from the bankers that it emulated and develop a risk management system to control the risks that were left over from its deals. Enron set up a separate division, Enron Risk Management Services (ERMS), to create the necessary tools both for its own use and for sale to its clients.

Enron's gas bank became a major division of Enron that came to be known as Enron Gas Services (EGS) and later Enron Capital and Trade Resources (ECT). Jeff Skilling left McKinsey & Company to join Enron and would become the Chief Executive Officer of EGS and later ECT. His success in those jobs would ultimately lead to his becoming CEO of all of Enron in 2001. Much of Enron's reputation as a world-class innovator comes from the creation of the gas bank and Enron's later efforts to duplicate that success in related markets, most notably electric power.

However, Enron planted the seeds of its own destruction in the process of becoming the center of the natural-gas universe. Its aggressive accounting practices and the use of special purpose entities (SPEs) have their roots in Skilling's operation.

When Enron entered into a long-term natural-gas contract with either a producer or a consumer, it faced the problem of how to account for that transaction on its accounting books. While it is easy to blame both Enron and the accounting profession for the path that Enron took and where it eventually led, the truth is that there is no entirely satisfactory way to account for complex deals that extend over several years. In an economically perfect world, the right thing to do is to book the profits from the deal at the time the deal is made and then, as the deal plays out and the value of the contract changes over time, use the mark-to-market process described earlier to determine any gains or losses. Recall that Ken Lay was an economist, so mark-to-market accounting would be the natural route for him to take.

The mark-to-market approach is standard operating procedure for a financial institution that invests in stocks. While a stock certificate looks like a fancy piece of paper, it is formally a claim against the future earnings of the company. Because most stocks that financial institutions own are actively traded, it is easy to determine the value of their holdings. If an investment bank is able to get a bargain of a stock, nabbing a block of a million shares from a nervous seller at a price of $20 per share, and then sees the price rebound to $21 per share by the end of the trading session, it can book a cool million in profit. Mark-to-market accounting, which is the standard practice for financial institutions, does not require that the shares be sold to book the profit; however, every day the new price of the shares must be taken into account in determining the profit or loss from the position. Today's gain can easily become tomorrow's loss. The $1 million that we made today when the stock closed at $21 could turn into a $2 million loss tomorrow if the stock falls to $19 at tomorrow's close.

MARK-TO-MODEL

The problem that Enron faced is that many of its custom contracts were very difficult to value—there was no price in an active market to use as a reference point. The alternative, which was also in common use on Wall Street, was to value the contract using a computer model, a process known as mark-to-model. Indeed, in many investment-banking circles, bankers would lapse into the illusion that computer-model generated prices were real prices and misleadingly refer to mark-to-model prices as mark-to-market prices. Enron not only fell into the same trap, but as its competition caught up with it and profits were harder to come by, it would also manipulate the models to its advantage.

Enron's use of mark-to-market (or model) accounting was rare among industrial firms, and it would take the accounting profession years before it would become a standard accounting practice. The immediate advantage that Enron gained from mark-to-market accounting was that it put a very positive spin on its earnings—something that a more conservative accounting approach would not. It also set a trap for Enron that many hedge funds (and people would come to regard Enron as essentially an enormous hedge fund) fell into. Many hedge fund disasters, such as the one that struck Long-Term Capital Management in 1998 and nearly brought world financial markets to a grinding halt, arise when a small hedge fund discovers a new trading strategy that works, generating huge returns on a relatively small initial investment. As the fund expands and others begin to emulate its behavior, profits shrink. In an effort to continue generating enormous returns, the hedge fund must take on increasingly more risk until it reaches the point where a few small mistakes are enough to make the fund blow up.

Enron's story follows the standard hedge-fund scenario, but with an important twist: The risks that Enron took in an effort to maintain its rapidly growing profits included engaging in legally questionable activities. The activities that have aroused the most suspicion are those related to its SPEs, and Enron first got into the SPE business in connection with its gas bank.

SKILLING AND FASTOW

The natural-gas producers that were most willing to make deals with Enron were those that desperately needed cash. While Enron may have had many things, spare cash was not one of them. In order to get the money needed to buy gas at bargain prices, it needed to team up with those who had it—banks and related financial institutions. The way to formalize the partnership in which Enron would set up the deal and the banks would provide the money was to create an SPE that got the banks' money to the natural gas producers in exchange for future deliveries of natural gas. This was a perfectly legitimate business deal that was similar to the SPEs used for movie distribution described in the Preface, except that natural-gas deals could last up to 20 years rather than the few months it takes a film to earn back its distribution costs.

These SPEs were a critical step in Enron's evolution. It was already beginning to develop major relationships with banks because of its need to manage the risk in its gas bank. It would use natural-gas futures contracts and a variety of interest-rate futures to lay off much of the risk from the pieces of contracts that it was forced to hold on either a temporary or a permanent basis. As its sophistication grew and, as mentioned earlier, the financial job market grew tighter, it was able to attract talent from banks to move to its Houston headquarters. In 1990, Enron's Skilling hired a bona fide financial wizard, a senior director from Continental Bank in Chicago, to lead the effort of constructing SPEs. His name was Andrew Fastow, and he would come to create the SPEs that would put more than $40 million directly into his pockets and set the stage for Enron's downfall.

4

The Downside of Rank and Yank

The arrival of Andrew Fastow at Enron in 1990 was what might be considered the final addition to Enron's solar system of management. It completed the triumvirate of Lay, Skilling, and Fastow—names that would in time become household words—and in some sense created the three major managerial stars within Enron. In total, they became Mr. Outside, Mr. Inside, and Mr. Inside's Insider. Compared with Kenneth Lay, who played golf with presidents, and Jeffrey Skilling, who was a business strategy visionary, Andrew Fastow was a relative nobody. If Lay were the Sun and Skilling the Earth, Fastow was something more obscure and tangential—more like the Moon. Indeed, even when he became chief financial officer (CFO) of Enron in 1998, few at the company knew who he was.

Rotating around these three were many others within the elite senior management solar system at Enron. Around Lay rotated Skilling, Rebecca Mark, and much earlier in Enron's history, Richard Kinder. Around Skilling rotated executives like the hand-picked Fastow and many rising stars from Enron Capital and Trade Resources (ECT), who composed in part his macho clan of executives known as "The Mighty Man Force." Many of these executives had risen through the ranks with Skilling and drove the success of Skilling's gas bank. In contrast, Fastow rotated around both Lay and Skilling, with a strong gravitational allegiance to Skilling and the corporate culture that he promoted.

Understanding these individuals—and the battles they sometimes fought for and against one another—only illuminates the dynamics of Enron's corporate culture and shows how it contributed so significantly to Enron's monumental failure.

For some at Enron, this culture was run by the Romans, who made sure they had the most intellectually bright Greek slaves around. There was always a huge salary, a bonus, stock options or stock, and perhaps even a half-dozen parking spaces monitored by security cameras for the Romans within Enron who were tight with Lay or Skilling. In many instances, the salary levels of the "slaves," even adjusting for the cost of living, did not live up to Wall Street standards. The myth at Enron, which spread across the whole enterprise, was that it was always possible to become a Roman if you battled long enough within the halls of its cutthroat meritocracy. It was not long, however, before the Greeks recognized exactly who the Romans were, and that their apparent freedom was not all it was cracked up to be.

Andy Fastow grew up in New Jersey and attended college at Tufts University, where he majored in economics and Chinese. At Tufts, he made his Houston connection by marrying Lea Weingarten, daughter of the owner of a prominent chain of Houston supermarkets. After he got his M.B.A. from Northwestern's Kellogg School of Management, he and his wife both worked at the Continental Bank in Chicago before they moved back to her hometown to work at Enron. Andy and Lea kept a low profile, living in the modestly affluent area adjacent to Rice University rather than in River Oaks, the much flashier home to Houston's business and sports elite, including Lay and Skilling. Only toward the very end of Fastow's tenure at Enron did he and his wife make plans to move to River Oaks.

Unassuming as Andrew Fastow may have appeared, he was tough and intimidating when confronted directly. He did not do well at cozying up to the analysts on Wall Street whose research (if one could call it that in retrospect) helped determine Enron's stock price. Subordinates at Enron who might question his tactics and apparent self-dealing feared that Fastow would have them fired on the spot or reassigned to dead-end jobs. Somehow, Fastow was able to build an empire of SPEs of dubious legal status without anyone at Enron, including its board of directors, standing in his way. Furthermore, Fastow installed himself as the manager of these SPEs, a role that required a waiver by the company of Enron's own code of ethics. From this position of power, Fastow was able

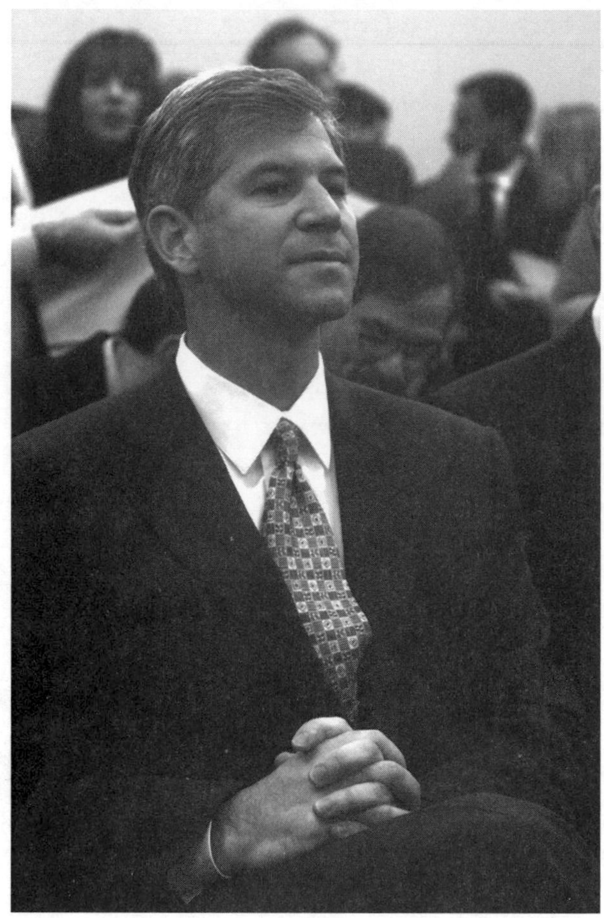

Former Enron Chief Financial Officer Andrew Fastow waits to testify on Capitol Hill on February 7, 2002, before the House Oversight and Investigations Subcommittee hearing on Enron. Fastow invoked the Fifth Amendment and refused to testify to Congress, saying, "On the advice of my counsel I respectfully decline to answer the questions." (AP Photo/Dennis Cook)

to funnel vast sums of money into his own pockets and into the pockets of those who assisted him. It is possible that if Enron had continued to prosper, Fastow's dealings could have gone unnoticed indefinitely; however, in 2001 Enron's fortunes would abruptly take a turn for the worse.

CORPORATE CULTURE

Enron's misdeeds are so egregious and its downfall so spectacular that it is natural to look inside the company, to examine its culture in an effort to see how things could have gone so very wrong. Attempting to analyze an organization from a distance is often a dubious proposition, even if media pundits do it all the time. In the case of Enron, however, there is reason to believe that its fate was largely the result of an extremely dysfunctional organization.

Superficially, Enron had much in common with other successful organizations. It strove for excellence and was obsessed not only with being the best but also with hiring the smartest people. Of course, who is "best" and who are the "smartest" are subjective notions. Alas, there is no guarantee that having what many in the industry would agree are the smartest people is a recipe for success. In early 1998, the hedge fund Long-Term Capital Management, with two Nobel laureates and several professors lured from the top universities, was regarded in many financial circles as having the smartest people. Whether it was because they were so smart or in spite of that fact, Long-Term Capital Management would set the standard for failure until Enron came along.

For all the influence that Jeffrey Skilling had on its operations and Andrew Fastow had on its finances, Enron was still very much Kenneth Lay's company. Kenneth Lay's personal philosophy would carry over to Enron as a whole. Kenneth Lay, an economist, believed in the power of markets; Enron prospered by creating new markets, and markets would serve as the model for Enron's internal structure.

One popular image of free-market economics is a smiling Milton Friedman spouting profound utterances such as "There's no such thing as a free lunch" (after a phrase actually coined by science-fiction writer Robert Heinlein). While all mainstream economists agree that free markets are fundamentally a good thing—even the liberal *New York Times* columnist Paul Krugman, an Enron adviser himself, would likely concur—they differ on how far that freedom should extend. If you ever find yourself annoyed at having taxes withheld from your paycheck, you have Milton Friedman, who helped design the withholding system in a moment of weakness, to thank for it.

FREE MARKETS FOR FREE MEN

The free-market guru whose thinking appears to have influenced Kenneth Lay (and, by extension, Enron) the most is Ronald Coase. Like Milton Friedman, Coase is an economics Nobel laureate who taught at the University of Chicago. While teaching at the University of Virginia, Professor Coase visited the University of Chicago for a dinner attended by the leading scholars of the University of Chicago economics department. Coase had just written an article that argued that the Federal Communications Commission (FCC) should not simply give away licenses to television and radio broadcasters, but should employ a market mechanism to sell them. The Chicago economists had thought that this was too much to ask of any market, but by the end of the evening Coase had convinced the lot of them that such a scheme would work.

What Coase had discovered was that many problems that economists had long felt were beyond the reach of markets and might only be solved by extensive government intervention could be solved if the government limited its intervention to assigning and enforcing property rights. The first problem that Coase tackled using this reasoning was related to pollution.

Traditionally, government had dealt with the problem of pollution by setting standards that placed uniform limits on the amount of pollution a power plant or factory could emit. Coase determined that an even better way to control pollution is to assign pollution rights and then let companies trade them. Similarly, the FCC should not control the airwaves, but auction the rights off and let broadcasters, cell phone operators, and others trade them.

Enron, as the emerging giant in the natural-gas industry, was very happy to see trading in pollution permits begin to surface in the 1990s. Facilities that use or convert to natural gas from oil or other fossil fuels will emit less pollution and will need to purchase fewer pollution permits. This gives natural gas a cost advantage credit for being friendlier to the environment. Indeed the expertise that Enron developed in natural-gas markets would spill over into the market for pollution permits, which was one of the next markets that Enron entered.

On a grander scale, the Kyoto Accords envisioned the market for pollution permits expanding internationally as part of a plan to place a global cap on the emission of greenhouse gases. Enron had sound business reasons to support the Accords. Still, many free-market economists failed to embrace the Kyoto Accords. This is because governments, and not the market, would determine at what level to cap emissions and how the permits are initially distributed.

Coase's idea formed the basis of a general belief that free markets worked only if the markets were available. Having only some markets in place was insufficient for capitalism to work its wonders; you had to have the right markets. Enron's formula for success, first demonstrated with its gas bank, was to become the provider of some of the right markets. As we shall see, it moved from natural gas to electric power to pollution permits to telecommunications to water and then started taking everything onto the Internet with its EnronOnline system. It cannot be said enough times that free markets were Enron's religion.

Enron's internal corporate culture reflected its brand of free-market religion. While Professor Coase is the acknowledged godfather of tradable pollution permits and the FCC's telecommunications auctions, that is not the work for which he first became famous and which earned him the Nobel Prize in economics. Much earlier in his career, Coase developed the theory of why firms exist at all. He found that certain types of transactions, particularly those involving cooperation and coordination, are too costly to leave to the market. Corporations, families, and other social institutions are able to achieve things within their protective shells that the market mechanism, at least in its current form, simply cannot. While Coase pioneered ways to extend the influence of markets, he also had the wisdom to understand where markets should not go.

The area where transaction costs for a company are often the highest is in the hiring and firing of its personnel. Unlike office products that can be purchased, used, and disposed of at will, workers can be costly to hire and even costlier to fire. While successful companies are always looking for ways to reduce the amount of deadwood in their employ, they tend to do so in a manner that will appear to outsiders to be as fair and reasonable as possible. Cynically, this may simply be done to minimize the number of lawsuits brought against the company, but it makes good business sense as well.

In a statement to shareholders in the 1999 Enron Annual Report, Ken Lay stated, "Individuals are empowered to do what they think is best. . . . We do, however, keep a keen eye on how prudent they are. . . . We insist on results." That, in a nutshell, described how Enron viewed its employees. Enron's corporate culture was essentially focused on two things: The first was profits and the second was how to make even greater profits. The firm didn't strive to create long-lasting business relationships and had little desire to be involved in anything that smacked of the low margins associated with retail-oriented business.

As a rapidly growing company, Enron had to commit considerable resources to recruiting personnel. New Enron employees could be divided into two categories: those who joined the firm directly after completion of their bachelor's or master's degrees and those who joined as seasoned industry professionals.

Seasoned professionals who were hired by Enron were typically individuals who were looking to enhance their careers and professional skills. They ranged from industry executives and managers looking to acquire enhanced financial skills to investment bankers and senior lenders seeking increased exposure to commercial transactions and risk management. The traders that Enron hired generally came to Enron to trade—although there are several instances where traders who joined the firm developed investment banking related skills.

Enron was a place where executives could, in effect, remake themselves for their next job after Enron. Former Enron employees are still in great demand in the energy industry due to their high level of trading and deal-making skills. Enron's popularity and soaring stock price encouraged other energy companies to follow its lead, and hiring its employees was seen as the quickest way to emulate it. As it would turn out, Enron may simply have been leading its competitors over the cliff with it.

Potential university recruits were interviewed on campuses by some of Enron's highest-ranking employees. The company targeted graduates from the top U.S. universities. The company also recruited undergraduates from top-rated engineering schools and universities with solid business programs. Enron actively recruited undergraduates majoring in mathematics, engineering, and science. Candidates with these majors, the company believed, tended to possess an above-average intelligence and a strong work ethic following years of demanding scholastic schedules and all-nighters before exams. In some cases, liberal arts majors were hired if they fit the Enron model, assuming they graduated at or near the top of their class and came off as being aggressive. Regardless of their academic backgrounds, candidates had to demonstrate a strong sense of urgency in everything they did.

Candidates also had to demonstrate that they could maintain high levels of work intensity over an extended period of time. Some have compared the work environment and high employee intensity at Enron to that of a top law firm, which is typically filled with brilliant young associates willing to do whatever it takes to make partner.

SUPER SATURDAYS

After an initial screening interview, job candidates brought back for a second interview attended one of the three to five "Super Saturdays" held between December and March at the Enron Houston office. Each candidate was interviewed for 50 minutes by eight different interviewers in succession with one 10-minute break. Between 200 and 400 candidates were interviewed during each "Super Saturday" session.

Candidates were judged in five to eight categories. Each interviewer rated the candidate in each category and assigned the person an overall rating based on the average among the categories. The categories that were used to evaluate candidates included the person's sense of urgency, innate intelligence, and problem-solving ability. The rankings were 1 (lowest) to 5 (highest). Typically, there was a minimum cutoff point around 2.5. Anyone with an average below that number would generally not receive an offer.

Offers were made to prospective candidates within two or three days of the weekend session. Approximately half of all candidates attending a "Super Saturday" session were offered jobs. Enron was predisposed toward candidates who expressed an interest in working as traders; however, it placed new employees wherever it needed them most. If Enron found that a candidate turned down an offer, the company offered more money in the form of a signing bonus or salary.

Like the big accounting firms and law partnerships, Enron preferred to hire top undergraduate and graduate candidates instead of more experienced employees, because they made for a relatively cheap and flexible workforce. These recruits rotated to new assignments every 6 to 12 months until they found a permanent assignment or were promoted. Graduate recruits were usually promoted to manager within two years of their hire date. As for business school graduates, if they weren't promoted to manager within that two-year period, they often quit to work for a competitor or an investment bank. Undergraduate recruits, if they were not promoted to associate within two years, often chose to go off to business school.

STANDARD OPERATING PROCEDURE

Despite all the effort that Enron expended in selecting the right people to hire into the company, it was quick to fire them. Enron evaluated its employees using a method that came to be known as "rank and yank." The "rank" part was standard operating procedure for a business like Enron. Most companies secretly divide their employees into groups both to determine raises and promotions and to document inferior performance that might serve as the basis for a future personnel action.

Enron employees were ranked every six months on the same 1-to-5 scale as new recruits; however, 15 percent of all employees were required to be in the lowest category (1), and they were yanked from Enron. To give the appearance of fairness, those yanked had until the next semiannual review to improve. In practice, however, with new waves of 15-percent yanks coming every six months, it was difficult for those in the bottom category to escape for very long, so they usually chose to accept a severance package rather than stick it out. Furthermore, those in categories 2 and 3 were effectively put on notice that they, too, were liable to be yanked within the next year. With half of Enron's workforce in serious jeopardy of losing their jobs at any given time, Enron has been described by many employees as having an absolutely cutthroat culture that pitted one employee against another. While there are estimates that up to 20 percent of companies in the United States use some form of rank-and-yank mechanism to clear out their deadwood—usually yanking the bottom 10 percent once a year—Enron's extreme form of rank and yank cast a constant shadow of insecurity over all but the most highly ranked employees.

It is clear that Enron's management regarded kindness as a show of weakness. The same rigors that Enron faced in the marketplace were brought into the company in a way that destroyed morale and internal cohesion. In the process of trying to quickly and efficiently separate from the company those employees who were not carrying their weight, Enron created an environment where most employees were afraid to express their opinions or to question unethical and potentially illegal business practices. Because the rank-and-yank system was both arbitrary and subjective, it was easily used by managers to reward blind loyalty and quash brewing dissent. Although Enron may have been praised by *Fortune* magazine as one of America's "most admired companies," its employment practices would be considered reprehensible by many of its peers. In the end, Enron's blind adherence to a misguided notion of how to apply market discipline to its internal operation would contribute greatly to its downfall.

5

A Market a Day Keeps the Debt Away (But Only Temporarily)

While Kenneth Lay provided the overarching vision for Enron, Jeffrey Skilling developed the means for implementing that vision. It does not appear to be a coincidence that the strategic model that Skilling ultimately used to grow Enron was the same one that consulting firms used to grow their businesses.

Before we examine how Enron grew during the 1990s, moving from its central position in the natural-gas markets to a similar role in electric power, pollution permits, and other commodities such as bandwidth, let's consider the industry that inspired Jeffrey Skilling. Originally, consulting firms were think tanks that made money by solving problems that their clients were unable to solve for themselves. Consulting firms would focus on technology problems, providing a more hospitable environment for the experts on their staffs than would be found at their client companies, who would only occasionally require their expertise.

Beginning in the 1960s, however, consulting took on a new face with the rise of firms that specialized in business problems—the management consultants. Among the most notable of this new breed was the Boston Consulting Group (BCG), founded in 1963 by Bruce Henderson. Like many of the founders of management consulting firms, Henderson was a business school professor. Rather than serve merely as a temporary labor pool for its clients, BCG and its contemporaries figured out how to turn sound strategic advice into a true product. They would start with an initial client—usually one of some prominence—to serve as a willing guinea pig. The consulting firm would develop a new technique for conceptualizing a major strategic problem for the client. (The actual work of implementing a solution to the problem was usually left to the client.)

The partners in these consulting firms designed their techniques so that they would be simple enough that fresh-faced business school graduates, who were paid a tiny fraction of what the partners received and were billed out to clients at a hefty premium, could administer the consulting product with a minimum of supervision. While the firm might well lose money on the initial assignment, as it applied the new techniques to dozens of new clients, few new costs would be incurred and the profits would roll in. In this way, the benefits of mass production came to consulting.

In the late 1970s, as Jeffrey Skilling was graduating from Harvard Business School, BCG's strategic vision that it applied to businesses with several product lines was all the rage. (These large businesses could also afford to pay hefty consulting fees.) Without going into the gory details, BCG's methodology included plotting all of a company's products on a two-dimensional grid. Its breakthrough idea was that a company should maintain a balanced "portfolio" of products along the grid, while avoiding placing any product in the sector that was labeled "dogs," those products with a small share of the market and little prospect of increasing it. The two most desirable types of products were "cash cows" and "stars." While cash cows had gotten too big to grow much further, they dominated their market in a way that provided the company with a reliable flow of earnings. Stars were even better; they not only brought in profits but were growing rapidly as well. The only problem was that stars could not be expected to shine indefinitely and a star did not burst on the scene spontaneously; rather, it had to be nursed into being. The cash from the cash cows was to be used as venture capital for the incubation of future stars.

BEYOND CASH COWS AND STARS

As corny as this methodology may seem, it was instrumental in the rapid growth of the General Electric Company during the 1980s and 1990s. Early in his tenure as GE Chairman, Jack Welch brought in a hot young consultant from the Boston Consulting Group named Michael Carpenter, much as Kenneth Lay brought in Jeffrey Skilling from McKinsey & Company several years later. GE embraced a variant of the BCG philosophy that might best be called "Be first, be second, or be gone." This philosophy was based on the observation that most cash cows and stars tended to be either the first or second largest firms making their products. Mike Carpenter also helped Jack Welch with the acquisition of Kidder, Peabody, an investment banking firm that was no better than fifth in any of its major product lines. GE had difficulties with Kidder from day one—Jack Welch considers the acquisition his biggest mistake—so Welch put Carpenter in charge of the investment bank. Had Mike Carpenter met this challenge, he would likely have become heir apparent to Welch's throne. Unfortunately, he presided over a trading scandal that ultimately led to his departure and the sale of Kidder, Peabody to PaineWebber. This story has a happy, if slightly ironic, ending. GE made a killing on the stock in PaineWebber that it obtained in exchange for Kidder, and Michael Carpenter went on to be Chairman and CEO of Citigroup's corporate and investment banking business, which is one of Enron's largest creditors.

At Enron, Jeffrey Skilling would come to employ a more modern business strategy known as "asset lite." Starting with the advent of junk-bond financing in the mid-1980s, cash cows were seen as no longer necessary to generate the cash that would fuel a company's growth. That was the job of investment bankers. In the highly competitive industries in which Enron competed, cash cows were almost impossible to find. With little control over market prices, most investments in hard assets, such as wells and pipelines, were bound to be dogs. As in consulting firms, the real money was to be made from people and their ideas, which is known as "intellectual property." Enron's product was "the market" and its profits were to be made by creating markets in as many goods as possible using natural gas as its model.

Jeffrey Skilling would not get the opportunity to put his strategy to work until 1997 when he would effectively gain control of Enron's day-to-day operations. Before then, Enron's day-to-day operations were run by Richard Kinder, who was the number two man at Enron and Kenneth Lay's right-hand man. Furthermore, Kinder was the Enron executive who negotiated the deal with Skilling that brought him into the company.

Kinder was the embodiment of the "old economy" approach to investing. He always demanded that there be a strong economic reason for investing in a project. When presented with a proposed deal sheet, he would automatically skip the executive summary and written justification and go immediately to the projected income and balance-sheet statements. Deals without a reasonable prospect of generating tangible profits never saw the light of day. Kinder preferred to acquire hard assets even if their purchase weakened Enron's financial position by loading it with debt and driving it into the hands of junk-bond financiers like Michael Milken. In most instances, though, Kinder showed a knack for improving the return on assets that Enron acquired or developed that made Lay loyal to his efforts.

When it came to personnel, Richard Kinder was "kinder" than Jeffrey Skilling. The old Enron actually tried to make its employees happy. Kinder was regarded as tough on the deals he approved, always using a very sharp pencil, but he was also regarded as a fair and prudent decision maker. With Kinder's departure, those days were over and the era of rank and yank would blossom under Skilling.

MORE ASSETS, BIGGER ASSETS

With Kinder's and later his replacement Rebecca Mark's guidance, Enron bought, built, or financed several large-scale assets, including the Teeside power station in Britain, several gas pipelines around the world, gasoline additive methyl tertiary-butyl ether (MTBE) facilities, and the Dahbol power plant in India. As we shall we, these last two acquisitions would come back to haunt Enron and ultimately contribute to Lay's selection of Skilling over Mark as his successor.

Richard Kinder left Enron at the end of 1996 and went on to found Kinder Morgan, which would compete with Enron. He assumed the post of Chairman and CEO of Kinder Morgan and even managed to take some of Enron's hard assets with him. He acquired Enron Gas Liquids, which was a public subsidiary that Enron had created as a growth vehicle for international asset acquisition and development, by outbidding six other suitors that included Mobil Oil. Although Kinder paid the highest price for the company, it was likely that he understood the true value of its assets given his intimate knowledge of every asset Enron owned.

At the time of Kinder's departure, Enron's natural-gas trading operation had left its infancy and entered a painful adolescence. The easy money from creating the market for natural gas had already been made by Enron, so the time came to look for similar opportunities in order to keep the money machine rolling.

In order to run a successful market, it is important that one understand the role that options play in a market. The most important option that a market can provide to its buyers and sellers is liquidity—the option to acquire or dispose of a position at will. (As we shall discuss later, in Chapter 9, it was Long-Term Capital Management's failure to appreciate the importance of liquidity as an option that led to its downfall.) Actively traded stocks on the New York Stock Exchange and Nasdaq are examples of highly liquid investments. Most of the time, shares of these stocks can be purchased and sold at or near the prevailing market price in a matter of seconds. This ability to get in and out in a hurry makes these shares more valuable. The existence of an active market provides each owner of the stock with a valuable "liquidity option." In other words, in a liquid market you can convert your investments easily into cash because there are many buyers. In an illiquid (or less liquid) market, it can take longer to get cash for the asset or investment. The stock market is pretty liquid; the auction market for antiques is less so because you have to wait until the auction houses hold their seasonal auctions, and the buyers who might want your antique desk may or may not be in the market for your desk at the time you are selling it. In a liquid market the opportunity to get the price you are looking for is greater than in a less liquid market—mostly because there are fewer buyers.

Michael Milken understood this when he created the new market for junk bonds. Even before Milken went into the business of helping companies issue junk bonds, he profited from creating a liquid market for the fallen angels that had been downgraded to junk. When Milken was finally able to create his own "original issue" junk bonds in the 1980s, having this secondary market in place helped him in three ways. First, controlling the "book" of business for the bonds provided him with valuable information on the current state of the market that he could legally use to maximize his profits in the market. Second, he could directly profit by serving as the middleman on most trades. The third and most subtle way that he benefited from this market was that its existence made junk bonds more valuable, making it easier to Milken to generate the enormous fees that came from underwriting their issuance.

LIQUIDITY PROVIDER

Enron's position as primary market maker in natural gas placed it in a similarly advantageous position as a provider of liquidity. One thing that Enron knew even before it started the market was that its creation would make natural gas contracts more valuable by making them substantially more liquid. The standardization of contracts, another Enron innovation, would also promote the liquidity of the market. The best way to cash in on the new market was to buy up natural-gas contracts at bargain prices and then sell them at a profit once the market was established.

Enron used its power in the marketplace to buy natural gas from financially distressed producers at bargain prices. As we noted earlier, this required that Andrew Fastow set up special purpose entities (SPEs) in order to finance these purchases and keep them off Enron's accounting books. Enron continued to expand its use of legitimate SPEs during Richard Kinder's tenure at Enron. In 1993, it joined up with the California Public Employees' Retirement System (CalPERS) to form the first of its *Star Wars* inspired SPEs, Joint Energy Development Investments, or JEDI (to be renamed JEDI I when JEDI II came along). Getting CalPERS in on the deal not only took the venture off Enron's balance sheet, it gave Enron new credibility. As the largest public pension fund and one of the largest institutional investors, CalPERS' seal of approval was extremely valuable. Professional money managers were often willing to take a loss on business that they did with CalPERS knowing that simply being chosen by CalPERS would open doors at other pension funds. It was the proposed expansion of the JEDI program under Jeffrey Skilling in 1997 that led to the creation of the controversial SPE known as Chewco, which would start Enron down the slippery slope of increasingly questionable SPEs.

The role of options in Enron's making of markets went beyond the liquidity that it provided to its customers. Because factors outside Enron's and the market's control would always affect the supply of and demand for natural gas, those who entered into long-term contracts would always desire some degree of flexibility. That flexibility would take the form of options that were written into Enron's deals. These embedded options were often difficult to value, but by drawing on Wall Street talent Enron initially was in a better position to value these options than were the traditional players in the natural-gas market. Once the market was established, however, other players learned how to value these options, either on their own or by hiring talent that Enron had yanked.

The bottom line for Enron was that the bulk of the legitimate profits from creating a new market would come in the first year or two of its existence. As producers and consumers would figure out how the market worked they would strike increasingly better deals, squeezing out Enron's profits in the process. Furthermore, there was nothing preventing other companies from getting into the same business of making their own natural-gas market. Enron did maintain a natural advantage by having the most trading activity flowing through it. A buyer or seller looking for a specific natural-gas deal was most likely to find it through Enron, just like a seller of antiques knows that the major auction houses such as Sotheby's or Christie's are where the bulk of the business is done by sellers and buyers. Enron earned its fee—known in trading vernacular as the spread—by catching natural buyers and sellers as they were entering or exiting transactions. (Think of the spread as a kind of commission that is built into prices—because Enron would always buy any contract at a lower price than it would sell it—rather than tacked onto them after the sale.)

A LESS THAN IDEAL COUNTERPARTY

For all of Enron's apparent success as a market maker, it did have an Achilles' heel. Unlike a stock exchange, where most trades are made directly between a buyer and a seller with the exchange only serving to facilitate the trade, every trade that passed through Enron was made directly with Enron. In legal terms, Enron served as the "counterparty" to every deal. The obvious advantage to this arrangement was that the purchaser of a long-term gas contract did not have to worry about the seller being unable to deliver. The less obvious disadvantage was that it did have to worry about Enron's ability to meet its commitments.

Enron's big problem here was that its enormous debt and lack of hard assets made it a poor choice for a counterparty by Wall Street standards. Even though Enron had emerged from junk status by the time it started its natural-gas market, it always remained at the low end of investment-grade companies. A significant financial setback (or the rating agencies getting wise to how it operated) would be enough to push it back to junk. Without an investment-grade credit rating, Enron was out of business as a market maker because no one would trust it to fulfill its obligations as a counterparty. Indeed, even with a low investment-grade credit rating, no one should have trusted Enron.

Wall Street firms that served as counterparties in financial markets were required to have high investment-grade credit ratings. This often meant that they had to set up special subsidiaries that locked their capital away from the parent. Enron not only lacked the capital to create a financially sound subsidiary to serve as counterparty for its deals, it had to resort to increasingly creative (some might say underhanded) means to get the capital to manage its inventory of contracts. If Enron did not ultimately obtain sufficient capital to support its market-making operations, it would likely have succumbed to competition from Wall Street. Once companies that dealt with Enron began to discern that Enron was more likely to default on deals than were Wall Street firms, the discounts that Enron would have to offer to keep their business would destroy the deals' profitability. Indeed, all that happened to Enron was that this process was accelerated when its financial woes began to surface in 2001.

In 1997, before Enron's problems surfaced, Jeffrey Skilling likely saw that the challenge he faced was how to make the nonrecurring profits from starting a new market into recurring profits. From an accountant's point of view, the profits that Enron made from the assets that increased in value because of the liquidity that the new market provided could be considered nonrecurring, so that they would not be incorporated into Enron's reported earnings. The way that Enron could make them recurring was for it to be continually in the process of creating new markets.

One obvious new market for Enron to create was one for wholesale electric power. Enron had a natural advantage entering the electric-power market because it was so similar to the natural-gas market. Both markets were for energy that flowed through a vast network and plants that burned natural gas and produced a significant fraction of all electric power, especially in states like California that had strict clean-air standards. Also, electric power was in the process of being deregulated on a state-by-state basis. The primary challenge that electricity posed was that, unlike natural gas, it could not be stored for later use. Enron not only was able to meet this challenge, it also was able to use it to its benefit by being in a position to take advantage of temporary shortages as they happened.

Enron clearly saw big opportunities in electric power. In its 1998 Annual Report there is a section called "Fortifying the Energy Franchise" that begins with the following statement of Enron's future path:

> As electricity prices in North America temporarily rose from $20 per megawatt hour to as much as $7,500 per megawatt hour in mid-1998, Enron recognized a need for new, flexible generating capacity that would be able to respond quickly to the market. Enron moved immediately to begin construction on 1,300 megawatts of peaking facilities in Mississippi and Tennessee that will begin commercial operation in the summer of 1999. In addition, Enron recently acquired gas-fired generating assets representing more than 1,000 megawatts, the majority of which is connected directly to, and is located less than 10 miles from, New York City. In addition to strengthening Enron's flexibility in dispatching natural gas, the plants produce reliable electricity for customers in one of North America's most energy-intensive markets.

Leaving aside for the moment Enron's foreshadowing of sky-high electricity prices in the opening sentence, the gas-fired generators that it acquired would fit into a bigger pattern of deception. Enron plays down the fact that the more than 1,000 megawatts that were acquired were not all within 10 miles of New York City—its own press release on this deal indicates that some of these megawatts were located in Camden, New Jersey, roughly 80 miles from the city. This omission is minor in comparison with the fact that Enron did not really acquire the assets because it lacked the capital to do so; instead, Andrew Fastow fashioned an SPE about which he boasted to *CFO* magazine, "We accessed $1.5 billion in capital but expanded the Enron balance sheet by only $65 m[illion]." Enron effectively acquired only half of the generating assets and hid virtually all of the debt.

Enron's direct and indirect acquisition of electricity generation facilities was the precursor to its creation of an electricity market. As noted earlier, the value of all such assets was likely to increase once that market for buying and selling electricity contracts was made liquid by Enron's new market.

BEYOND ELECTRICITY

Enron did not stop at electricity; it continued to create new markets for everything from tradable pollution rights to metals, pulp and paper, and other industrial commodities such as specialty chemicals. It even got involved in the market for swap and options contracts based on the weather that manufacturing or agricultural businesses could use to hedge spikes in temperature that might affect the costs to purchase power or negatively impact crop yields. As temperatures spike upward in summer and fall in winter, utilities also potentially needed a hedge against the weather. Or so Enron thought—thanks to an idea that some Enron sources say Jeff Skilling's brother Thomas, a weatherman in Chicago, suggested. But, of course, even reliable data as pristine as the National Weather Bureau's may not be sufficient to attract buyers and sellers to a new market, or to build one from scratch.

The electricity market was a big success for Enron, but the other markets were more questionable. In particular, the paper market was so different from the energy market, even though paper production used vast amounts of energy, that Enron had difficulty making the market work.

The real revolution at Enron occurred when it discovered the Internet. While its 1998 Annual Report portrayed it as the dominant energy company in America, the 1999 Annual Report, which came out in early 2000, presented Enron as the champion of the "new economy," the dot.com to end all dot.coms. If there was ever a sign that the days of the Internet bubble were numbered, this was it. A market for bandwidth trading was deemed visionary at the time not only by Enron but also by many others, particularly with share prices for Internet-driven businesses going through the roof. Though the infrastructure for a bandwidth market was hardly what Enron had encountered in natural gas or electricity, Enron's visionary Jeff Skilling was unashamed to tell analysts in late 2000 that it was the next big thing for Enron. He argued it might drive Enron's share value up to $126.

How wrong he would be. There were two conflicting strategies at Enron: To invest in energy, telecommunications, and other technology businesses required that Enron assume more debt to finance these enormous investments. The other strategy—"asset lite"—required that it have the creditworthiness to do business with counterparties in the financial markets. These conflicting strategies—and the accounting methods that were used to conceal more than they revealed—only put Enron on a collision course with the inherent contradiction of its own vision as a company.

6

Enron Goes Online

In the letter to shareholders that kicked off its 2000 Annual Report, Enron stated proudly:

> We are participating in a New Economy, and the rules have changed dramatically. What you own is not as important as what you know. Hard-wired businesses, such as energy and communications, have turned into knowledge-based industries that place a premium on creativity. Enron has been and always will be the consummate innovator because of our extraordinary people. It is our intellectual capital—not only our physical assets—that makes us Enron. Move our assets to another company, and the results would be markedly different.

The letter went on to detail both the Internet-related ventures it had initiated and the hard assets it had liquidated during the year.

Jeffrey Skilling's asset-lite strategy was ahead of the curve (but not too far ahead), and Enron was turning into the ultimate Internet company at a time when investors couldn't get enough of them. The New Economy had such a profound effect on the way Enron viewed itself that CEO Jeffrey Skilling replaced his vanity license plate, which read WLEC (world's largest energy company), with a new one, WMM—or "We make markets."

The watershed moment that kicked off the Internet boom was the initial public offering (IPO) of Netscape Communications in August 1995. Netscape had developed the first Web browser that was designed for commercial use. (Its predecessor, Mosaic, was developed as a noncommercial research tool by Netscape cofounder Marc Andreessen at the National Center for Supercomputing Applications at the University of Illinois.) To help establish its market presence, the browser was distributed free of charge over the Internet, and only commercial users were required to purchase licenses for the software. Large companies would typically purchase site licenses that allowed Netscape's software to run on any of their computers for a single annual payment. While licensing fees brought some revenue into Netscape, they did not come near covering the costs required to develop and promote the company's products.

What set Netscape's IPO apart from the vast majority of IPOs that preceded it was that not only was Netscape unprofitable at the time of the IPO, but it also had no immediate prospect of profitability. Generally, companies that went public had to already be operating at a profit and have reasonable expectations of remaining profitable indefinitely. Until a company was profitable, it would have to live off the funding made available to it from venture capital firms or other private sources of funding. Netscape's IPO was a phenomenal success and its stock price soared immediately after the offering. Venture capitalists and investment bankers sought to repeat the success of Netscape as many times as possible and would take their companies public earlier and earlier and still see their stock prices soar. That companies could turn admittedly half-baked ideas into billions of dollars in paper profits overnight was a warning sign that all was not right in the new economy.

The old-economy approach to valuing a company's stock was based on an estimate of how much the firm could expect to generate in profits over its lifetime. These projected earnings (or a related measure of profitability, such as dividends or cash flow) were then adjusted to take into account how long one had to wait to receive them and how uncertain they were to materialize at all. In this fundamental approach to valuing stocks, pioneered by Benjamin Graham and David Dodd and made popular by the likes of Warren Buffett, every dollar that one paid for a stock had to be returned to the investor with interest at some point in the future.

Given that the Internet was still in its infancy, it was impossible to forecast when a company would become profitable, how great its profits would be, and how long they would last. In the new economy, ideas were what mattered, so they, and not future profits, increasingly determined stock prices. For a while, in the absence of profits analysts looked at current revenues in their efforts to justify stock values, but as the Internet bubble grew, even that approach was abandoned by the more popular Internet touts. Even the most deluded investors seemed to be aware that only a minuscule fraction of the Internet-related companies that were coming to market would ever show a profit, yet each was being valued as if it were the next Microsoft. It was like everyone was buying lottery tickets that were priced so high that even the winning ticket might not pay enough to cover its cost.

DREAM COMPANY

Enron gave every appearance of being the dream Internet company. It not only had substantial profits and revenues, but they were growing rapidly as well. And, if only by accident, it had a presence in two of the hottest areas of the new economy: business-to-business electronic commerce and broadband communications. It would turn out that both Enron's profits and revenues were illusory, but amid the mania that drove the market for Internet-related companies, these shortcomings were easily overlooked by all but the most critical analysts. What helped the analysts at the major investment-banking firms to avoid peering too deeply into Enron's finances was that Enron's continuous appetite for financing—both for itself and for its SPEs—generated substantial fee income. Analysts knew that looking askance at Enron in public would jeopardize those fees and their jobs. Indeed, Chung Wu, an analyst at UBS PaineWebber, sent an e-mail containing this warning to

73 of his clients: "Financial situation is deteriorating in Enron. . . . I would advise you to take some money off the table. . . . Waiting to make a decision would cost you a fortune." After a copy of the e-mail landed at Enron, Wu's bosses sent out the following correction: "I hereby retract Mr. Wu's statements. . . . UBS PaineWebber has a strong buy recommendation on [Enron] stock." Wu was fired the same day "for violating firm policy concerning electronic communications," according to UBS PaineWebber, a policy that requires firm approval for "correspondence being sent to 10 or more persons."

Enron's rare position as a profitable Internet company, however, put it in a bind. In order to keep its stock price at a stratospheric valuation, it had to continue to grow both revenues and profits. It was becoming commonplace for companies that missed their earnings numbers by even a single cent per share to fall by 50 percent or more on the announcement. As it became clear that companies were manipulating their earnings estimates to make sure they could meet expectations, Wall Street began to expect firms to achieve even higher "whisper numbers." Companies that failed to clear these higher hurdles would be punished by the market even if they beat analysts' estimates. Failure to make its numbers was a problem for Enron because not only was the wealth of Enron's leaders closely tied to its stock price but, as we shall see later, so was the viability of the company. Enron had become addicted to growth and, like a strung-out junkie, would do *anything* to get its next fix.

Before we chronicle what Enron had to do to stay in the good graces of the stock market in the next chapter, it is worth taking a closer look at Enron's one possible success (it is still too early to tell for certain) in the Internet world, EnronOnline. This Internet offering by Enron is notable because it was not a part of Jeffrey Skilling's grand plan; rather, it was an unexpected innovation that Enron's culture is credited with fostering. In fact, because Skilling initially opposed the project and at one time opposed use of the Internet by Enron employees for security reasons, the creators of EnronOnline developed it without Skilling's knowledge until it was near completion.

FLIP THE SWITCH

EnronOnline is considered to be the brainchild of Louise Kitchen, who was head of Enron's European gas trading division, a position moderately high up Enron's management hierarchy but nowhere near the top. Kitchen, on her own initiative and without letting top executives in on the deal, oversaw the design and implementation of EnronOnline in just seven months. The project required 380 programmers, traders, and managers, many of them working nearly around the clock, who were borrowed from other projects. Similarly, computer hardware was borrowed to get EnronOnline up and running. While at some companies this may have been grounds for dismissal, Enron rewarded the developers of EnronOnline handsomely for taking the initiative, and Louise Kitchen was promoted to president of EnronOnline.

EnronOnline was officially launched in November 1999 and it grew rapidly. In February 2000 EnronOnline was processing 1,000 transactions a day worth almost $450 million, and by July 2001 it had grown to 5,000 transactions a day worth $3 billion. Moving all this business from costly direct interaction with traders to online access through the Internet may have saved Enron money, but it was worth even more as a public relations coup that made Enron into a prime Internet success story. It was also a principal reason that *Fortune* magazine continued to select Enron as the most innovative company in the United States for a period of six straight years, from 1996 to 2001.

The basic structure of EnronOnline is shown in Figure 6.1. With this system in place, Enron made trading its standardized contracts as easy as point and click.

The kind of entrepreneurial autonomy behind the creation of EnronOnline was an Enron virtue that helped make it the darling of the business press. Have an idea for a new business or process? Be prepared to oversee it yourself if your plan is deemed worthy. Employees in the company's analyst-training program were measured every six months on their "intellectual curiosity" as much as anything else. Top executives were constantly recycled into new positions, and youth, just as at the Internet start-ups, was no barrier to assuming huge responsibility.

Despite the buzz that EnronOnline generated, its effect on Enron itself was not unambiguously positive. As we will explain, it very likely reduced the profits that Enron made from many of its trades. In the short run, which is where Enron needed to get its profits to satisfy Wall Street's expectations, Enron could make up for lower margins with the higher trading volume that EnronOnline brought to it. In

1. User logs on to view a customized set of markets in which he/she wants to buy or sell.

BUY SELL
3. To buy or sell, user clicks the price button. A screen pops up on which user can change the volume on an order or simply click "OK."
2. Buy and sell prices are displayed side by side. The "spread" (margin between the bid and the offer prices) is visible on all deals and can change by the second.

4. The deal's done. Settlement, transportation, and other logistics are handled off-line.

Figure 6.1 **EnronOnline**

Source: Global Change Associates.

the long run, however, margins would likely continue to narrow without an offsetting increase in volume. Although Enron's competitors, most notably The Williams Companies, quickly brought out their own online trading systems that further drained profits from Enron, it is questionable whether any of them had the capability to design such a system from scratch.

CHANGING SEAS

EnronOnline represented a fundamental shift in how Enron did business. It starting its trading business by emulating Wall Street's most profitable trading operations. Even now, most corporate bonds and many other financial instruments do not have their true prices posted on the Internet. (Any prices that are posted or faxed to clients usually apply to only very small quantities and even then they are subject to change without notice.) Instead, deals are made the old-fashioned way using the telephone. The broker determines whether the caller is buying or selling and then quotes only the price that the caller needs to know to make a deal. For example, buyers are quoted only the offer (sale) price, and sellers are quoted only the bid (buy) price. By keeping this information to themselves, dealers can widen the spreads between their purchase and sale prices without passing this information on to the market. As a minor concession to their customers, brokers in such markets rarely charge commissions, as these are dwarfed by the spreads. This arrangement may well hurt the market for bonds by making them less liquid—and less valuable—than securities that are openly traded with both their bids and offers listed. Still, Wall Street and its customers generally find this arrangement suits their needs, and Internet-based markets for most bonds have been slow to catch on.

In moving its business online, Enron gave up some of the spread yet continued to forgo commissions, unlike a typical online securities broker such as Ameritrade. Also, Enron continued to be the counterparty to all transactions. Hence, all the bids and offers posted on EnronOnline represent deals with Enron on the other side. If Enron had stuck to its core competency of energy trading this might have worked out well, but Enron ended up making markets in 1,800 different products that spanned dozens of markets (see Figure 6.2). As a middleman, however, Enron stayed out of traditional financial and commodities markets because those markets were regulated by either the Securities and Exchange Commission (SEC) or the Commodity Futures Trading Commission (CFTC). Enron attempted to exercise its vast political influence through

Transacts in 13 Currencies and Over 1,800 Products

Commodity Types

- U.S. Natural Gas
- U.S. Power
- Canadian Natural Gas
- U.K. Natural Gas
- Oil and Refined Products
- German Power
- European Coal
- Nordic Power
- U.S. Metals
- Liquefied Petroleum Gas (LPG)
- U.S. Weather
- International Coal
- Emissions
- Asian Crude and Products
- Austrian Power
- Dutch Power
- Swiss Power
- Bandwidth
- Petrochemicals
- Credit Derivatives
- Australian Power
- Sea Freight
- Spanish Power
- European Weather
- Australian and Japanese Weather
- Belgian Natural Gas
- Japanese Aluminum
- Pulp and Paper
- Plastics
- Argentine Natural Gas

Auctions

- Emissions (U.S.)
- EnBank Virtual Storage (U.K.)
- Pipeline Capacity

Options

- Continental Power
- Nordic Power
- Nuclear Outage
- Knock-in Call Options

Figure 6.2 **Product Offering on EnronOnline**

Source: Enron/Global Change Associates.

contributions to assure that the markets that it entered would not fall under the control of regulators.

EXPANSION FOR WHAT?

This expansionist view accelerated Enron's tendency to enter markets in which it had little expertise. Of prime importance to a successful market maker is having more knowledge of a market than those who trade with you. Enron's rapid expansion into new markets virtually guaranteed that its willingness to make deals might place it at the mercy of more knowledgeable insiders.

While the contributions of EnronOnline to Enron's profits are uncertain (Enron did not break them out in its financial reports), it certainly pumped up Enron's revenues, which is what Wall Street analysts had become more focused on during the Internet boom. Much of the spectacular 150 percent increase in revenues from 1999 ($40 billion) to 2000 ($100 billion) is due to a quirk in how accountants compute the revenue for energy trades. If an investment bank purchases a security and then sells it, only the spread between the sale and purchase price counts as revenue. For trades in energy products and other goods that are not considered financial instruments for accounting purposes, however, the entire amount of the sale can be booked as revenue. These legitimately inflated revenues combined with some improperly inflated ones that we will discuss shortly enabled Enron to rise to fifth on the Fortune 500 in 2002 (based on 2001 revenue results). By then, it did not matter because Enron had already declared bankruptcy. EnronOnline was among the first of Enron's holdings to be sold off by the bankrupt firm in an effort to reorganize itself into a viable going concern. It should come as no surprise that EnronOnline was purchased by one of the world's strongest financial institutions, UBS Warburg, a division of the Swiss superbank UBS AG. In contrast to Enron's borderline junk credit ranking, UBS is a high-investment-grade bank that ranks consistently among the top 10 safest banks in the world in *Global Finance* magazine's annual survey and is a well-respected financial counterparty. Louise Kitchen and much of her management team were included in the deal that brought EnronOnline to UBS Warburg.

EnronOnline's new home may make it a more credible counterparty, but its future success is not guaranteed. As they say, you can tell the pioneers by the arrows in their backs. Just as Netscape, Lotus, WordPerfect, and Novell did not prevail by dint of being the first to market with their products (all of these firms ultimately succumbed to Microsoft), EnronOnline faces tough competition in the future. Economists with state-of-the-art laboratories at the California Institute of Technology, Harvard, Carnegie-Mellon, Arizona, George Mason, and other major universities are developing a new generation of "smart markets" that are specifically aimed at the heart of EnronOnline's market, the production and transmission of energy. Smart markets can function as intelligent deal makers that can systematically explore billions of possible deals before settling on the best ones. The Federal Communications Commission already has a mandate from Congress to use smart markets to auction off cellular phone licenses, and both IBM and Hewlett-Packard are among the technology companies that have active development programs underway. One can only imagine what Microsoft is doing in this field.

NEW ECONOMY DISASTER

While EnronOnline gave all the outward appearances of success, Enron's other high-visibility foray into the new economy was an unmitigated disaster. That was its broadband communications venture. Enron may have achieved dominance in the energy markets while its stodgy competitors could only watch in awe and envy before deciding they had no choice but to try to catch up. But in broadband communications, where fiber-optic cables serve as a virtual fire hose that gushes voice and data, everyone had come early to the party and the appetizers were quickly devoured. Given the competition that Enron was to face in broadband, it ended up taking an act of God to keep Enron from following many of its fellow new-economy companies down the tubes in 2000.

7

Broadband Is a Costly Mistake

Early in the famous novel *Catch-22* by Joseph Heller the incredible story of Chief White Halfoat is told. The Chief claims that members of his family are blessed with an uncanny attraction to oil. Wherever they move, oil can surely be found underneath their tents. Over time, this blessing turns into a curse as his family is surrounded with geologists and oilmen wherever they go. In the end, the Chief himself is the sole survivor of his family and only because he is drafted and sent to fight in Europe.

While Heller uses this story as one of many examples of the absurdities of life that culminate in the ultimate catch-22—that the only way to get out of flying bombing missions is to ask to leave on the grounds of insanity, but the very request to leave proves that one is sane—Enron's apparent successes themselves provided the seeds of its future failures. While even the best companies have to manage their way out of failure from time to time, Enron repeatedly found itself incapable of taking the right action at the right time.

Jeffrey Skilling was certainly aware of the fact that while Enron was able to achieve uncontested dominance in the natural gas and wholesale electric power markets, eventually its competitors would catch on and Enron would have a real battle on its hands. On Skilling's desk sat a plaque with the letters "IRIS" stamped on it. IRIS was an acronym that stood for: "First They *I*gnore You, Then They *R*idicule You, Then They *I*mitate You, and Then They *S*teal from You."

The problem that Enron faced while it was building the market for broadband communications was not limited to intense competition from several other energy companies who wished to cash in on Internet mania, but was due to competition from the companies that were developing the broadband capabilities that Enron wished to trade, most notably the now-bankrupt Global Crossing. As in the previous markets that it created, Enron began by acquiring hard assets expecting that its new market would increase their value. This time, however, was different because so many others were playing the same game. The big telecommunication companies were in it, too, and they were getting boatloads of financing from the same investment banks that funded Enron.

Broadband communications became the darling of Wall Street because the technology was the key to developing high-speed Internet access. The natural reasoning was that if the Internet could be (or, in retrospect, could appear to be) such a big success when most homes connected to it were using relatively slow dial-up connections, just imagine how wonderful it would be if everyone could connect at high speeds. In the past, such connections were available only to businesses. They had to pay high monthly fees for the privilege of having a "fat" (or broadband) connection to the Internet.

The biggest problem in moving to a broadband world was that the existing telecommunication infrastructure was incapable of doing the job. The existing network of telephone lines was particularly problematic because the DSL (direct subscriber line) technology that could facilitate broadband communications was not without its glitches.

Central to any plan to extend broadband Internet connections to every home was the need to increase the capacity of the information superhighway that connected cities and countries. For years computer industry pundits, including Robert Metcalfe, who invented Ethernet, were predicting that use of the Internet was growing so rapidly that very soon the entire network would become gridlocked, rendering it virtually unusable. While the occasional outbreak of a computer virus or worm would clog parts of the network, it seems that new capacity was added quickly enough to avert a total failure of the network. If every home were to have a broadband connection, the copper wire that constituted most of the existing network would have to be supplemented with fiber-optic cable.

Fiber-optic technology, which uses tiny pulses of light that can transmit a million telephone conservations at once over strands of pure glass that are thinner than copper phone line, is one technology that truly deserves to be called revolutionary. For the businesses that became involved with building networks of fiber-optic cable, it may have turned out to be too revolutionary.

The problem facing broadband is best illustrated by a television advertising campaign used by Qwest, a company that, although it may sound like a breakfast cereal while its corporate slogan "ride the light" appears to come from the science-fiction book and movie *K-PAX*, is really a leader in broadband communications. This campaign features a series of commercials in which a traveler arrives at a restaurant or motel "in the middle of nowhere" and finds that every song or every movie ever made is instantly available to him or her through the wonders of fiber optics. These commercials gloss over the obvious point that neither Qwest nor any other broadband communications company has licensed the rights to this vast amount of intellectual property and that thousands of intellectual property owners might not want to ride the light with Qwest at a price they would consider reasonable. Fiber-optic cables might bring enormous capacity to the Internet, but without a flood of new traffic to flow through them they are virtually worthless.

KILLER APPS

As the year 2000 began and the concerns about the Y2K bug subsided, demand from bandwidth along the Internet was being spurred by a "killer app" known as Napster. Napster was a file-swapping service that provided a central directory to files that resided on millions of personal computers around the world. Napster users would allow access to the files that they wished to share with others on their computers in exchange for access to the computers of other Napster users. That Napster facilitated connections from one user to another made it a peer-to-peer network.

The most popular files on Napster where those that contained tracks "ripped" directly from CDs and compressed to occupy a few megabytes of space. (Depending on the quality of one's equipment and how well the compression was done, the loss in quality could range from unnoticeable to glaring.) While it could take an hour to transfer a single track using dial-up lines, with a good broadband connection the transfer time could drop to seconds. Napster not only increased the demand for broadband connections to the Internet but also increased traffic along the major highways of the Internet as music flowed across state and country boundaries. With Internet traffic booming, billions in financing to build fiber-optic networks streamed out of Wall Street at bargain interest rates.

Then the problem of intellectual property reared its ugly head. Napster's founders interpreted the copyright laws as allowing the file transfers that its system facilitated, much as the owner of a book, CD, or videotape is free to lend his or her copy to others. The recording industry, however, did not see things Napster's way, and neither did the courts. Although the injunction that shut Napster down in July 2000 may have only slightly dented the growth rate of Internet traffic because file swappers had other ways to acquire music over the Internet, it increased the doubts that had arisen over what was seen to be the future killer app for the Internet that would gobble up bandwidth, Video on Demand (VOD). Enron was among the first companies to see the promise of VOD over the Internet. Just days before the injunction came down against Napster, Enron inked a 20-year pact with Blockbuster, the video-rental giant, that would allow Blockbuster to "rent" movies using VOD technology over Enron's fiber-optic network, which it had modestly named the Enron Intelligent Network. That deal quickly collapsed, with Enron claiming that Blockbuster was unable to secure the rights to enough movies to make the venture viable.

ENRON AND QWEST

If neither Enron nor Qwest could have imagined just how difficult it was to get Hollywood to put its movies on the Internet, especially after what Napster had failed to do for music, at least they had each other. The broadband market that Enron developed allowed companies to trade bandwidth, which is the use of some of the capacity of a fiber-optic cable for a specific period of time. This market turned out to be a complete bust, with even Enron's own accounts showing them hemorrhaging millions of dollars. Superficially, the market appeared to be doing business. Each month hundreds of trades would appear to take place. But Enron may only have created the illusion of liquidity. Although all the facts are not yet in, it appears that virtually all of the trades that went through Enron's broadband market could have been designed to artificially inflate revenue. On March 29, 2002, the *New York Times* reported that Qwest was being questioned by the Securities and Exchange Commission (SEC) about possible "sham" trades that it had done with Enron.

Enron's alleged broadband mischief could be much larger than simply making its market look more impressive to help attract business. The SEC was specifically interested in a $500 million broadband swap between Enron and Qwest that was made just as the third quarter of 2001 was coming to a close.

The idea behind sham trading is fiendishly simple. Suppose that you and a friend are both running antique businesses and at the end of the year you find that you are losing money and you don't want your spouses to find out that business is going so poorly. Each of you could take a piece of Shaker furniture that you had bought earlier in the year for $500 and agree that each piece of furniture is now worth $2,500. By merely swapping the two pieces of furniture, you could each appear to have made $2,000. You each did this by selling something you have bought for $500 at a price of $2,500. The problem if no one is willing to pay $2,500 for each of those antiques (and no one may even be willing to pay $250) is that neither of you has *really* made any money.

(To make matters worse, all of the "profit" exists only in accounting terms; no cash was generated by the transaction.)

Enron and Qwest are suspected of doing essentially that, only on a much grander scale, in order to book quick profits that they could then show off to the financial markets. A Qwest spokesman, the *New York Times* reported on March 29, 2001, said the company "bought much more than network capacity from Enron; it had also obtained power supplies, spare network conduits and the right to place its equipment at Enron sites." According to the *Times*, he declined to discuss how Qwest valued each element of the deal, but stated, "We paid what we believe was fair market value for the package we bought." Enron also declined to discuss specifics.

But even these questionable shenanigans are still only the tip of Enron's financial iceberg. Getting into broadband turned out to be anything but an "asset lite" strategy for Enron. The company had to spend billions of dollars to become a player in a market that was dominated by telecommunications companies. This money came from SPEs that would make a Wookie cry.

A very interesting thing about Enron is that even during a time when the Internet bubble was bursting, taking the Nasdaq Composite index from a high of 5,000 in March 2000 down to below 2,000 the following March, Enron's stock actually moved up a bit. While Nasdaq was falling over 60 percent, Enron stock rose from about $70 per share to $80 per share, having reached a high of around $90 per share in the interim. Some other broadband players had only minor declines in share prices, but Enron stood as a giant in the marketplace.

As it would turn out, the high price of Enron stock was not just an outward sign that the company was doing well. Given that Enron had used shares of its stock as the backing for many of its deals, a high stock price was crucial to the firm's survival.

BUYING TIME

One reason that Enron thrived for so long was that it continued to make money in the energy markets. Indeed, while tech stocks in general were languishing on Nasdaq, the perennially unloved utilities in the Dow Jones Utilities Average had become the new stars of Wall Street with Enron as their standard-bearer. The strong U.S. economy spurred growth in electricity consumption, while environmental concerns had severely limited the construction of new power-generating facilities. This increase in demand without a corresponding increase in supply was most pronounced in California, which had partially deregulated its electricity markets in 1996. The part that remained regulated was the retail market, where except in the San Diego area prices to consumers were frozen. Historically, California's two big utilities, Pacific Gas & Electric and Southern California Edison, not only served consumers but also owned the plants that generated the electricity that they sold to them. As part of deregulation, California's utilities were forced to sell their power plants to other companies (many of them based in Texas) and then buy that electricity on a day-to-day basis.

With consumer electricity prices frozen and the California economy growing rapidly, fueled in large part by the technology boom, Californians were using a lot more electricity. With little new supply and no way to lock in the old prices, California's big utilities had to pay more for electricity. In particular, during peak consumption times, such as around dinnertime on hot summer weekdays, electricity could easily cost 100 times more than its normal price. To put things in perspective, the $7,500/megawatt-hour price for electricity that Enron points to with apparent glee in its 1998 Annual Report means that the cost of electricity for running a typical 1,200-watt window-model air conditioner for six hours during the peak period in the evening is more than $50. Although consumers were not forced to pay $50 a day for each air conditioner they used (and hundreds a day more to run their refrigerators, televisions, etc.), the utilities that served them were, and under deregulation they had no choice. These utilities did have some industrial customers who were willing to shut down during peak times in exchange for lower electricity rates, but there were not nearly enough of them to make up for the growth in demand.

California's retail market was not very fertile ground for the type of energy trading that Enron did. By the time the millennium rolled around, Enron had liquidated most of its electricity-generating assets as its focus shifted to broadband. Hence, Enron owned no electric-power generators in California. It was involved in various ways with the industrial power market in California, but that represented only a tiny fraction of the entire market. Enron's competitors had a much larger presence, so the halo effect of the windfall profits that they got from selling electricity in California may have kept

Enron's stock from falling with the rest of the Internet companies. Enron had nothing to do with running the California power market, which was the job of the California Power Exchange. The rules of the Exchange were the result of political haggling and as part of the deal that was reached prohibited long-term power contracts that might help producers and consumers manage the risk of an energy price shock.

ELECTRICITY SHORTAGE HAUNTS ENRON

Whatever temporary benefit Enron may have gotten either directly or indirectly from higher electricity prices that began in California and ultimately spread to the rest of the western United States, the ill will that high prices and electricity shortages created would come back to haunt it. Many Californians believed that the power companies fabricated the electricity shortages for their own economic gain. Indeed, the head of California's Public Utility Commission, Loretta Lynch, testified before a Senate subcommittee that Enron used phony trades similar to those that it is believed to have employed in its broadband market to create "phantom congestion" at key points in the California power grid and generate more phony profits for itself.

In its alleged efforts to manipulate the California electricity market, Enron once again turned to *Star Wars* for the name of one of its strategies. In the "Death Star" strategy, apparent congestion would be created on the two main lines connecting northern and southern California, path 15 and path 26, which Enron would then be paid to relieve. Other strategies to manipulate the electricity market were given cute names like "Get Shorty" and "Ricochet" (see the Enron File 11 on p. 209). The separation between legally advantageous trading in a market and illegal market manipulation is very fuzzy, and so the use of complex trading strategies by Enron and the other power companies operating in California does not necessarily imply any wrongdoing by them. Still, public disclosure of these ominously named strategies would contribute to a public-relations nightmare for Enron and its ilk.

While we may never know how large a role, if any, Enron had in creating California's energy problems, neither it nor the other energy companies would continue to profit from them indefinitely. As the year 2001 began, California may well have been at the bottom of Enron's growing list of worries.

8

Enron Takes on Water

The first four months of 2001 would mark the end of the party for energy companies that were profiting from high wholesale electricity prices in California and its neighbors. Enron's woes, however, would stretch far beyond California to failures in its forays into international markets. Not only would Enron find itself without any cash cows that could pump much-needed cash into it, but every major bet that it made was turning into a dog. Clever accounting may have provided Enron with paper profits—with EnronOnline providing the vast majority of those—but cold, hard cash remained in short supply.

As we noted in the previous chapter, California did not provide a natural habitat for Enron because its half-hearted efforts at deregulation were not the kind of free-market environment in which Enron's market-making prowess could be fully exploited. Indeed, any efforts that it might make to gain some degree of control over California's electricity markets could easily be construed as illegal market manipulation. Enron may have faced some challenges in the "People's Republic of California" (as conservative critics have been known to refer to it), but it would have even greater challenges abroad. For Enron, everything was beginning to go wrong at once.

The problems with the California electricity market emerged in stages. May 22, 2000, is usually given as the day that the state officially moved into crisis mode, for that was the first day that the California Independent System Operator (ISO), the manager of California's power grid, declared the first Stage 2 power alert. This alert required some of California's businesses to curtail their electricity consumption until the alert was rescinded. The summer of 2000 would see several more Stage 2 power alerts as well as sky-high wholesale prices for electricity.

Normally, California would have no power problems in winter because its warm climate required far more summer use of cooling than it did winter use of heating. The high electricity demands of the summer of 2000, however, caused many electricity-generating facilities to skip all but the most urgent maintenance procedures in order to meet the peak demand on what the California ISO pronounced as its "No Touch Days." By the winter heating season, a significant number of California's larger facilities were closed for maintenance.

California experienced its first Stage 3 power alert, which warns that it may impose rolling blackouts, on December 7,

2000. While blackouts were averted on that day, the move to Stage 3 marked the beginning of a serious power emergency and brought federal regulators into the picture. Reluctantly, the Feds imposed a flexible rate cap of $150 per megawatt-hour at a time when the going rate had risen to an average of $1,400 per megawatt-hour (or, to use the earlier example, about $10 to run an air conditioner for an entire evening). The enormous cash drain placed on Pacific Gas & Electric and Southern California Edison was pushing both of them toward bankruptcy, and that prospect along with legal action taken by the State of California raised the possibility that the power generators might not receive payment for the power they sold.

Everything came to a head in January 2001. Unexpected generator outages combined with a reluctance of generators to supply electricity for which they would not be paid led to rolling blackouts on January 17 and 18. The high-flying energy stocks in the Dow Jones Utilities Average tumbled, falling over 17 percent in the first two weeks of January on bankruptcy rumors. The utilities survived the month, but the California Power Exchange did not. California continued to limp along through the winter, with more rolling blackouts in March and the bankruptcy of Pacific Gas & Electric soon to follow.

As the summer of 2001 began, wholesale electricity prices stabilized for a time and then began to drop rapidly. The last power alert of the year was announced on July 3. By the end of the summer, prices returned to their precrisis level. The summer had been cool, but the disagreement as to what caused the crisis and why it went away remains heated.

GOING INTERNATIONAL

As grim and steeped with politics as the California power crisis was, it was a picnic for Enron compared with the problems it was facing in India. While Enron's involvement in the California electricity market was largely peripheral, the company took center stage in India as lead investor in the Dabhol power project, reputed to be the largest power project in the world.

Like most large American corporations, Enron viewed international expansion as critical to maintaining its high growth rate. One reason that companies welcome international expansion is that it helps them to diversify risk. Even with globalization providing increasingly strong economic linkages among countries, many economic problems are local in nature. By locating in as many places as possible, a company reduces its proportionate risk stemming from a disaster that might occur in any one location.

The U.S. firms that had been most successful in expanding internationally were those whose products have mass appeal. Coca-Cola is a prime example of a company whose signature product is readily marketed to a world audience. Fast-food franchises and pharmaceutical companies have also found that they have little problem marketing their products around the world because of their intrinsic appeal. Enron's big products—markets—were a harder sell. Even in the United States, the center of the world capitalism, the energy markets in which Enron specialized had only started the progress of deregulation within the last quarter century. With deregulation in the hands of individual states, the process could well stretch out for another quarter century. Some European markets, the United Kingdom in particular, were also moving toward freer energy markets. Still, in countries that had yet to develop democratic institutions, markets were a very tough sell.

Enron began to take international expansion seriously in 1993 with the creation of Enron International. This new division was the idea of Rebecca Mark, who was to become its first president. If you have not figured it out by now, Enron's management for all their drive and passion were not particularly exciting or appealing people (and they were also men). Rebecca Mark, in contrast, led a prime-time soap opera existence.

Rebecca Mark was a striking woman with honey-blonde hair whose ability to get her way in a business dominated by men earned her the nickname "Mark the Shark." She was provocative, known for wearing three-inch stiletto heels as part of her attention-getting designer wardrobe. She had a lot in common with Kenneth Lay, coming from a rural Missouri background and a Baptist family. She also had something in common with Jeffrey Skilling: an M.B.A. from Harvard Business School. But she did not follow the consulting path that he did. After a brief stop at a Houston bank, Mark worked for a natural-gas company that Enron purchased. Ken Lay is said to have liked her style and paved the way for her to lead Enron's international expansion. Of course, Ken Lay also liked

Rebecca Mark, chairman and chief executive officer of Enron International, posed in her office in October 1997. Mark was in charge of developing energy projects in places throughout Europe, Asia, and Latin America. (AP Photo/Brett Coomer, File)

Jeffrey Skilling, and so it was natural for a kind of sibling rivalry to develop between them—the kind you find on soap operas.

A large part of Mark's ability to make deals was that by making a big impression she was not easily forgotten; indeed, people were happy to see more of her. Adamant about traveling only by Enron's private jets, Mark and her entourage would circle the globe in search of new assets for Enron to acquire. Once she found the assets, she had what it took to close the deal. Rebecca Mark's moment of glory came in India.

BLACK HOLE IN INDIA

On its surface, Enron getting into the India power market looked like a good idea. The demand for electric power grows most rapidly in countries that are moving up in the ranks of the world economy. For example, South Korea's transformation into an industrial power was accompanied by a huge increase in its power consumption. India, with over a billion people—many of them well educated—and its most rapid growth still ahead of it, made it an appetizing market. Furthermore, a successful project in India would serve as a beachhead for the rest of Asia, which also had excellent growth prospects. Enron had found a prime location, the port city of Dabhol on the Arabian Sea, where it would partner with General Electric and Bechtel on a two-stage power project in which it would hold the majority interest. The first stage was an oil-burning generator and the second, larger phase would burn Enron's favorite fuel, natural gas. Although India itself was energy poor, oil and gas from the Arabian Gulf countries could easily reach it by tanker. As part of the project, Dabhol was to upgrade its port to accommodate the increased shipments of fuel. Of course, Enron would arrange the long-term deals for getting Dabhol a stable supply of oil and gas.

The arguments that could be made against getting involved with India were compelling. Historically, India has not taken kindly to capitalism, and the Bhopal disaster of 1984 certainly did not make the prospect of an enormous industrial project an easy sell on political grounds. Indeed, the Dabhol project created civil unrest that has led Enron to be accused of human rights violations for its alleged role in the violent suppression of dissent.

The efforts to get the project off the ground that began in 1992 were laced with frustration. Ken Lay even enlisted the aid of Bill Clinton's Commerce Secretary, Ron Brown, for a visit to India in January 1995 to keep the deal from collapsing. Despite political pressure from the United States, the deal with India fell apart later that year, causing Enron to seek $300 million in damages. Near the end of 1995, Rebecca Mark rode to the rescue, getting the deal out of the courts and back on track. This grand coup sealed Mark's business reputation and gained her new prominence both inside Enron and in the business world at large. She made the cover of *Forbes* in 1998, and the first stage of the project was completed in 1999. Many honors would be heaped upon her, including seats on the Board of Overseers of Harvard Business School and the Advisory Board of the Yale School of Management.

Unfortunately, by the time Dabhol was operational, it no longer made economic sense. (Many, including analysts at the World Bank, thought that it never made sense.) There are estimates that power from the plant cost four times as much as from other sources of electric power in India. India's government-run utility, just like California's two big private utilities, could not pay its bills. As Enron's luck would have it, this default also occurred in January 2001. The Bush administration was now enlisted to help an old friend, "Kenny Boy," and sent Colin Powell to talk to the Indian government in April 2001. Diplomatic efforts to limit the damage to Enron continued up until the day it declared bankruptcy, and then it was too late.

While Rebecca Mark had skillfully acquired a variety of assets for Enron, mostly in the energy field, she would next turn to a new market for Enron, water. Like natural gas, water flows and can be stored; however, it is fundamentally different because it is far less valuable. Indeed, in many areas, water is essentially free. In addition, the pipes and canals through which water flows have more restrictions on who can use them than do natural-gas pipelines.

AZURIX

In a scheme that seemed to come more from an episode of *Pinky & the Brain* than from the Harvard Business School, Enron planned to buy up the world's water with Rebecca Mark making the deals that would give them global dominance. It was becoming apparent to Ken Lay, however, that Enron's future was to be in trading, Jeffrey Skilling's asset-lite strategy, rather than in the accumulation of hard assets, which was Mark's forte. In 1998, Enron spun off a water company called Azurix, with Rebecca Mark as its chairman and CEO. Enron retained an interest in Azurix and Rebecca Mark retained her position on Enron's board. Azurix was now free to purchase assets without the debt required to purchase them appearing on Enron's balance sheet. Azurix started out with a single, very expensive asset, a small British water company called Wessex Water. In 1999 Enron raised

$695 million by taking Azurix public; however, Azurix needed Enron's financial backing (and high stock price) to stay in business given the way its deal was structured.

At the time, Azurix thought that it could use Wessex Water as a model for how to run a water business in developing countries, but it was wrong. In June 1999, Enron bid $438.6 million to win a 30-year concession to run five areas of Argentina's Buenos Aires province. Enron's bid was far higher than the bids of its competitors. Executives at Azurix learned that the water concession in Argentina was in worse shape than they had thought, and that strong labor unions were influencing the prices customers were being charged on their water bills.

Problems also emerged with contaminated water in Bahia Blanca, Buenos Aires, that cost Azurix $5.4 million in revenues. Overall, Azurix and its investments in water assets around the world became a textbook case of how Enron would do deals just for the sake of doing them, but without doing the homework necessary to ensure their success.

Azurix began to unravel quickly. In November 1999, the company announced that it was firing a third of its workforce in Houston and London in order to cut costs. The Wessex acquisition became a fiasco when government regulators slashed the rates that Azurix received for its water. Rebecca Mark finally admitted in June 2000 that the performance of the Wessex Water acquisition had "underwhelmed our expectations, dramatically." Mark resigned as

CEO of Azurix on August 25, 2000, blaming the British government for the company's failure in that country.

Jeffrey Skilling ultimately won out over Rebecca Mark when she was forced to resign as head of Azurix in August 2000. She would liquidate all of her Enron shares, giving her, by some estimates, $82 million in proceeds if the shares she sold before she left were included. How much of this she gets to keep has yet to be determined because even though she escaped Enron before disaster struck, she is included in many of the class-action suits filed against Enron. As for Wessex Water, it was sold by Enron in March 2002 to a Malaysian company for only $777 million, far less than the $1.9 billion Enron paid for it.

SKILLING ON TOP

In February 2001, as the bedlam described in this chapter was breaking on all fronts, Ken Lay handed the reins of Enron over to Jeffrey Skilling. Lay made Skilling president and chief executive officer of Enron, while retaining the position of chairman of the board. If all went well, Jeffrey Skilling would likely become chairman within a year or two. All did not go well.

Skilling may have managed to outmaneuver Mark for the job of CEO, but her legacy lived on in Dabhol and Azurix. These operations would prove to be too visible to hide—the whole world knew that Azurix was a failure and that Enron was not getting paid for its Indian power—and their resounding losses and a market that no longer supported Enron's stock price would trigger the avalanche that would ultimately bury Enron. "If a firm loses a billion here and a billion there, pretty soon it becomes material," notes Professor Harold Bierman of the Johnson School of Management at Cornell University. "It is not clear how buying a water company enables a corporation to trade water contracts on a worldwide basis."

9

From Arrogance to Bankruptcy

The Enron that Jeffrey Skilling took charge of in 2001 was not the company that he had envisioned as a consultant to the firm. True, Enron had become the poster child for the new economy with an online trading operation that looked like it would redefine how markets worked, but Skilling had also inherited a portfolio of assets that was an increasing burden on Enron. While Skilling was the champion of the rank-and-yank system that set tough, even unreasonable, performance goals for Enron's workers, he lacked either the will or the capacity to put Enron's acquisitions to a similar test.

At the heart of Enron's problems was Kenneth Lay's misguided trust in the power of markets. Enron may have been organized in a way that fostered innovation, but it also lacked focus and direction. The extremely competitive atmosphere and freedom to pursue new ventures within Enron may well have spurred innovation, but it led to a company with a hodgepodge of assets and strategies. The people who might have brought focus to the company, such as Richard Kinder, either left or were systematically purged and replaced with others, like Andrew Fastow, whose knowledge of finance lay in making deals rather than imposing controls. Although Fastow would win awards for his role as an innovator at Enron, some questioned whether he was competent to fill the critical oversight functions that were a part of a chief financial officer's job. Unquestionably, Enron had spun out of control under Kenneth Lay and Jeffrey Skilling, and the damage went far beyond being involved in too many losing deals.

Jeffrey Skilling would be CEO and president of Enron for all of six months. Skilling may have been unfortunate to have the calamities described in the previous chapter occur as he has taking over the company; however, his own actions and words would cast serious doubt on his suitability for the job.

Weeks after Skilling took the job, he did not see his face on the cover of *Fortune* magazine, but rather saw the words "Is Enron Overpriced?" An article with that title by Bethany McLean expressed the discomfort that some investors and analysts had concerning the high price of Enron's stock. It traded at nearly 55 times its annual earnings, which was more than twice the earnings multiples of its competitors. The article focused on Enron's lack of transparency; in other words, no one seemed to know just how it made its money. Such articles are common for high-flying companies, but usually in those cases the question was how long rapid earnings growth could continue. For Enron, the question was "Is this company for real?" It would turn out to be a question that would not disappear, and the doubts that surrounded the company would start to weigh on its stock price.

OVERPRICED?

On April 17, 2001, Enron released its financial results for the first quarter of 2001. The results looked healthy enough: Earnings were up 18 percent from the same quarter in the previous year, and revenues were up a staggering 280 percent. When Enron would submit its detailed numbers for the first quarter to the Securities and Exchange Commission (SEC) the following month, it would be clear that Enron's earnings were not translating into real cash. That things were not entirely peachy at Enron was also being reflected in its stock price. Enron, which had traded near $80 per share when Skilling become CEO, had fallen 25 percent to $60 per share.

Enron conducted a conference call both by telephone and over the Internet at 10 A.M. to discuss the results with those who followed the company. A typical conference call involves top executives taking turns putting the best spin on the reported numbers and their company's future prospects, followed by a question-and-answer session. Tough, even outright rude, questions are common, especially for companies, like Enron, that have attracted the attention of short sellers. As we noted earlier, hedge funds might want to sell shares of a company short to hedge the risk from a stock they own. Professional short sellers, however, are like opportunistic lions that run alongside a herd of wildebeests in hopes of turning the slowest and weakest into their next meal. Their short sales are direct bets that the stocks they sell will go down in price so they can repurchase them at a profit. A short seller lucky enough to have sold Enron stock short at $90 per share in August 2000 (near its peak of about $90.60) could buy it back at $60 per share in April 2001, giving a profit of $30 per share. It was in the interest of short sellers to spread their pessimism to others in order to drive the price of the stock down further. Understandably, companies are not fond of short sellers, especially the aggressive ones.

On the conference call, Richard Grubman, managing director of Highfields Capital Management in Boston, asked Skilling when Enron's balance sheet, which was not included in its press release, would be available. Skilling replied that it would be released as part of next month's filing with the SEC. Grubman was dissatisfied with this answer and remarked, "You're the only financial institution that can't come up with a balance sheet or cash flow statement after earnings."

Skilling then sarcastically replied, "Well, thank you very much, we appreciate that." Openly expressing annoyance was enough of a misstep, but Skilling then went over the line with the final word of his response: "Asshole."

DEFINING MOMENT

While this obscenity was directed at Mr. Grubman and other short sellers, Skilling's offensiveness would not be lost on the analysts who were Enron's cheerleaders. The enormous fees that Enron generated for the investment banks that employed the leading analysts likely overshadowed any questions about Skilling himself. They were also in denial about the possibility that Enron might be withholding its cash-flow numbers because it had something to hide. Still, the seeds of doubt had been firmly planted and would grow over the coming months.

This would be the defining moment of Skilling's presidency. Now it was obvious to all that Jeffrey Skilling did not get along well with others. Even tough CEOs like Jack Welch were expected to have a good-natured and jovial side. A CEO who could not quickly come up with a comic retort to defuse a tough question would at least be skillful enough to take evasive action. While Skilling may have viewed his unwillingness to suffer fools gladly as a sign of strength, others would see it as bringing his competence into question.

Two weeks after the earnings announcement, on May 2, Enron vice chairman J. Clifford Baxter would resign to "spend more time with his family," according to an Enron press release. Little notice was taken of Baxter's departure. Leaving the company via the "ejector seat" of the vice chairmanship was nothing unusual. Baxter's vague reason for leaving Enron was a standard executive euphemism used by those who are unhappy or have been forced out. Still, Baxter's departure troubled workers within Enron who viewed him as the conscience of the company. As Jeff Skilling's friend and colleague, Baxter knew what Enron was doing and is reported to have clashed with Skilling over a number of issues, but Baxter would not live to tell his story.

When the numbers that Richard Grubman had asked to see were filed with the SEC in mid-May they did not look good. At the same time that its reported earnings for the first quarter were $425 million, its operating activities had cost it even more than that—$464 million—in cash. Grubman's instincts were right, and Enron's wounds were starting to show as its stock continued its slow downward spiral.

Skilling's brief tenure as CEO continued on a rocky course and he did little to help himself. His lack of diplomacy showed at a technology conference in Las Vegas on June 12 where, according to the account given by the *New York Times*, Skilling joked, "You know what the difference is between the state of California and the *Titanic*? At least when the *Titanic* went down, the lights were on." Californians were clearly not pleased with Enron. Several days later in San Francisco, as he was entering the Commonwealth Club of California to speak on the state's energy crisis, a protestor threw at pie at him.

In July 2001 Skilling presided over another earnings announcement, and this time earnings were up 40 percent over the same quarter a year earlier. But Enron's host of problems finally began to surface in the numbers that it presented to analysts and the press. Its overall revenues were down slightly from the previous quarter; as fast as EnronOnline was growing (Enron was repeatedly criticized for not breaking out separate revenue numbers for its divisions), the growth was not fast enough to compensate for Enron's problems in broadband communications, Azurix, Dabhol, and California. The stock continued its descent and was trading below $50 per share when second-quarter earnings were announced.

No obscenities were uttered at this 10 A.M. conference call; however, when CEO Jeff Skilling was asked about what was going on with an entity related to Enron by the name of LJM Capital Management, all he said was, "A couple of real minor things."

BALANCE SHEET CONCERNS

That Enron still failed to provide analysts with either a balance sheet or other useful details was starting to concern them. More information would be provided to the SEC, and then only because that was a requirement that Enron could not avoid. The 10-Q form that Enron filed on August 14, 2001, indicated that while Enron's earnings were increasing (on paper) to $823 million, the cash it lost from operations had now zoomed over a billion dollars to $1.337 billion. That day, however, Enron's deteriorating financial situation was overshadowed by the shock of Jeffrey Skilling's resignation.

Enron's press release included the following statement from Skilling:

> I am resigning for personal reasons. I want to thank Ken Lay for his understanding of this purely personal decision, and I want to thank the board and all of my colleagues at Enron.

CEOs of large corporations are exceptionally driven people. They are never quitters, because a quitter could in no possible way endure the years of struggle required to reach the top. It was virtually unheard of for a CEO to quit suddenly for undisclosed personal reasons after only six months on the job. Skilling would repeatedly deny that his resignation had anything to do with what was going on inside Enron, but he found few, if any, believers in his story. Skilling's departure remains a big mystery in the Enron saga, but it would come to be just one of many mysteries. Skilling was clearly not having a good time at Enron—days when its stock would rise were few and infrequent. The company he ran was not the same as the one he had hoped to create. He was hated. He had good reason to want to leave, especially given what he should have known about what went on at Enron.

It is not clear that Skilling considered the impact his action would have. He would not be able to simply slink away from Enron, because his departure spooked both Wall Street and Enron employees. (As the world would later learn, an Enron vice president with some knowledge of what was really going on inside Enron would send Ken Lay a seven-page memo the next day that spelled out her concerns.) Skilling would come to describe the days after his resignation as the worst of his life.

In an effort to restore confidence in the company, Ken Lay reassumed the position of CEO. That no replacement for Skilling had been groomed to fill the position highlighted the suddenness of his decision to resign and the toll that its competitive culture had taken on its pool of executive talent.

PEP TALK

Ken Lay gave pep talks and sent upbeat e-mails (see the Enron File 6 on p. 201). Those e-mails would come back to haunt him. Because many Enron employees had massive holdings of Enron stock in their 401(k) retirement plans and indirectly through their employee stock options, the falling stock price was making them poorer and destroying morale. Lay's e-mails would tout the stock, at one point telling them that he thought it was "an incredible bargain." The problem was that until Skilling's departure Lay had been systematically disposing of large quantities of Enron stock. According to one of several class-action lawsuits filed against Lay and other Enron insiders who sold stock, Lay had sold over $100 million worth of stock in the 18 months before his e-mail campaign began. Lou Pai, who at one time or another had been the head of many of Enron's subsidiaries, was the leader of the Enron pack with over $350 million in alleged stock sales. Altogether, according to the civil suits, company insiders sold more than $1 billion in Enron stock. To make matters worse, for administrative reasons employees could not sell the Enron stock in their 401(k) plans for a few weeks during the crisis. There were suspicions that the lock-up was an effort by Enron management to prop up the stock price by keeping employees from joining the stampede of sellers.

With Skilling's resignation, the slow, steady decline of Enron's stock began to accelerate. The events of September 11 would temporarily shift the world's attention away from Enron, but its troubles came back into focus with the release of its third-quarter financial results on October 16. Enron finally appeared to be coming clean to the world. It took a $1.01 billion write-down to reflect the deteriorating condition of many of its businesses, especially the broadband communications business. This contributed to a third-quarter loss of $618 million. On the surface, it appeared that Ken Lay was taking the tried-and-true approach of airing all one's dirty laundry at once to get it out of the way. Indeed, he claimed that the new results would "find anything and everything that was a distraction and causing a cloud over the company."

But the real attention-getter was a $35 million partnership charge related to a special purpose entity known as LJM Capital Management that was run by Andrew Fastow. Documents related to LJM were leaked to the press, but their contents would not be available to the public until the Powers Report was released the following February. What little information about LJM and related SPEs that did leak out indicated that Andy Fastow had a very serious conflict of interest, and some wrongdoing may have occurred. Although the true size of Fastow's monetary compensation from the SPEs would come out later, it was rumored to be several million dollars. Some observers speculated that the partnerships had been set up to supplement Fastow's pay so that Enron, which had problems with executives leaving, could retain him. Shortly before the loss from LJM was announced, Andy Fastow was removed from any involvement in the SPEs that he had created for Enron.

Enron's downfall was like a slow-motion train wreck that played out for weeks in the business pages and eventually became a feature on the network nightly news programs. Whatever the true nature of Enron's problem, one thing was clear: If the ratings agencies downgraded its outstanding bonds to junk status, the company could not continue its usual business. Depending on the circumstances, it would either have to be taken over by a stronger company or file for bankruptcy. As noted earlier, in its trading businesses Enron was not like a normal broker who would match buyers with sellers. On each transaction Enron was a counterparty, serving as the buyer for every seller and the seller to every buyer. Without an investment-grade bond rating, Enron could no longer be a viable counterparty for new business—it would no longer be relied upon to deliver on its side of the contracts it wrote. If that was not bad enough, much of Enron's financing depended on its continuing ability to maintain an investment-grade credit rating. Any ratings downgrade that brought it below investment grade to junk might require it to pay off all of that debt. Enron lacked the funds to do so, making bankruptcy the only option. Even worse, many of the SPEs that it set up were backed by Enron stock, and if the value of the stock fell sufficiently, Enron was required to put up more stock, which it also did not have.

ANOTHER LTCM?

Once Enron's third-quarter results had been digested, concerns were raised on Wall Street that Enron would turn into another Long-Term Capital Management (LTCM). This was actually a very optimistic assessment of the situation. Three years earlier, in August 1998, LTCM had nearly collapsed because the market turmoil caused by the Russian debt crisis dried up the market liquidity that the hedge fund counted on to exit (and profit from) its positions. LTCM was essentially taken over by a syndicate of Wall Street investment banks that had the time and capital to unwind LTCM's positions (and make a profit for themselves in the process).

The situation that LTCM faced, however, was very different from Enron's predicament. LTCM invested almost exclusively in publicly traded securities; some of them were a bit obscure, but Wall Street was familiar with the securities in LTCM's portfolio. The only reason that LTCM had frightened the financial markets was because its positions, which were financed with loans from its brokers, were so large.

LTCM was easy for Wall Street to understand because it operated according to a unified vision that came out of the popular theories of its Nobel-laureate partners, Robert Merton and Myron Scholes, that were taught in every business school. Think of the financial positions that they constructed, and would profit from until the Russian problem surfaced, as being made of standard Lego pieces. When the Russian crisis hit, it was as if their Lego creation had been left outside in the Siberian winter and frozen together. This made the banks from which they had borrowed nervous, and so they wanted some of the pieces that they had lent LTCM back. When LTCM was unable to pry enough frozen pieces loose, the banks simply confiscated LTCM's creation, waited for it to thaw, and then threw LTCM back a handful of pieces. No one, except for some of LTCM's junior partners who borrowed heavily to buy into the company, went bankrupt, and the world's economy was unharmed by the whole affair.

In contrast, Enron was without a coherent vision and was doing things in a way that did not entirely make sense to Wall Street. They did not buy Lego pieces from the store; they injection molded their own custom pieces or new types of pieces that the market came to regard as being standard. Not only was it not entirely clear how all their pieces fit together, it was quite possible that no one else would have any use for some of the pieces. With LTCM, it was very quickly apparent what the hedge fund had created and how to undo it. Even months after Enron went under, no one really knew what sort of monster it created. This uncertainty about what Enron had done quickly affected the shares of any company that did business with it. A contract with Enron was increasingly unlikely to be honored, and how a bankruptcy court might handle it was anyone's guess.

Enron's stock was at $33 per share at the time the third-quarter loss was announced and dropped in half, to $16, over the following two weeks. Even with Enron now down over 80 percent from its high and its future in doubt, 10 of the 17 investment analysts who followed the stock rated it a "strong buy." Only Prudential's analyst gave it a "sell" rating. The biggest daily loss in that period, $5.40 per share, came on October 22 when the SEC announced that it was probing the SPEs created and managed by Andy Fastow. It would be followed by another loss of $3.38 two days later when Ken Lay fired Fastow.

Fastow's firing came as the government was uncovering the extent of his involvement in Enron's SPEs, most notably those known as LJM and LJM2. His fees had exceeded $40 million and some of his subordinates at Enron who helped him set up the SPEs were made millionaires. At this point, Lay had no alternative but to get rid of Fastow.

IN SEARCH OF A WHITE KNIGHT

The Enron drama for the month of November involved the quest for a white knight to save it before the ratings agencies lowered the boom and cut its credit rating to junk. As the month began, Enron's bonds had dropped sufficiently in price that their yields were comparable to some of the worst junk bonds. Credit ratings services that used objective computer models to rate credit, such as KMV Corporation of San Francisco, had already effectively downgraded Enron to junk. Moody's, Standard & Poor's, and Fitch all relied on human analysts to rate credits, and these analysts' bosses were getting calls from Enron begging them not to downgrade it. (Possibly because of the flak it caught for the Enron episode, Moody's would see the virtue of objective rating methods and acquired all of KMV early in 2002.) In the expectation that its sources of credit would soon be curtailed, Enron drew down all of its credit lines and started negotiations with two major banks, J.P. Morgan Chase and Citigroup, that were its largest creditors. As they say, owe the bank a little money and it's your problem; owe them a lot of money and it's their problem.

The only company to emerge as a serious candidate to acquire Enron was its crosstown rival, Dynegy. For all the grief that Enron had given Dynegy in the past, it was poetic justice that Dynegy be in a position to control Enron's destiny. With Enron's finances in a state of total disarray and its CFO in a state of disgrace, Enron was unable to present a clear picture to any buyer of what it might be buying. On November 8, in the midst of serious discussions with Dynegy, Enron officially corrected its financial statements for the past four and a half years, erasing the profits that had drawn investors into the company and substantially increasing its debt. The fact that the accounting firm that audited Enron's statements, Arthur Andersen, would have signed off on them in the first place drew Andersen itself into the investigation surrounding Enron. To make matters worse for Andersen, the firm had been accused of being lax as auditors and had paid millions of dollars of fines in the past as a result.

Despite all the problems that swirled around Enron, Dynegy reached a tentative deal to purchase the company for $8.9 billion on November 9. But Dynegy quickly found that even the restated financial statements could not be trusted. At first, Dynegy tried to renegotiate a better price for Enron, but those talks finally broke down on November

28. With all prospects of an Enron bailout gone, the ratings agencies finally threw in the towel and downgraded Enron to junk status immediately. Because of Enron and Ken Lay's close ties to the Bush administration, there was no way the U.S. government could bail Enron out without charges of corruption being immediately leveled at the presidency. As expected, bankruptcy quickly followed, with Enron filing for Chapter 11 protection from its creditors on December 2.

As the Dynegy deal fell apart, Enron's stock plunged to below \$1 per share and would no longer qualify for listing on the New York Stock Exchange. On the remote possibility that Enron might successfully emerge from bankruptcy, Enron shares continue to trade for pennies a share on the "pink sheets," a market for stocks that cannot qualify for exchange listing.

The most human face of Enron's fall were the many workers from below the executive ranks who had invested their entire 401(k)s in Enron stock and would see their retirement nest eggs, which may have been worth as much a million dollars just months earlier, vanish. Even larger amounts were lost in Enron's employee stock ownership plan. While sound financial management would dictate that retirement assets should be adequately diversified, the combination of Enron's aggressive matching of 401(k) contributions that went into its stock and Ken Lay's reassurances that all was well at Enron made it easy for many employees to ignore the conventional wisdom. Besides, at companies like Microsoft employees who loaded up on company stock were now multimillionaires, and Enron was going to be at least as good as Microsoft.

PRICE TRIGGERS PULLED

On November 28, 2001, with Enron stock trading at below $4, the ratings agencies lowered Enron's credit rating to below investment grade, which accelerated the payment due of $690 million in debt. This new obligation was already on top of an avalanche of cash or collateral that it owed to investors who were part of two other SPEs, the Osprey Trust and the Marlin Trust (a trust related to Azurix), totaling $2.4 billion and $915 million respectively. These obligations had price triggers that had been set off by Enron stock dropping below $59.78 on May 5, 2001, and below $34.13 on September 5, 2001. Each of these price triggers, in effect, was another bullet of debt that Enron had to endure if it were to remain standing. Time was running out for a company that was hemorrhaging badly.

When it declared bankruptcy Enron immediately fired 4,000 workers, and more job losses would follow. Many employees learned by voice mail that they had been terminated. The shabby treatment that the rank-and-file workers received from Enron management would sting even more when they learned that shortly before Enron declared bankruptcy it had provided top management with enormous bonuses ostensibly to keep them from jumping ship while Enron reorganized. Ken Lay was optimistic that Enron could emerge from bankruptcy as a smaller, stronger company. Few others saw it that way. With class action lawsuits galore filed against the company and rafts of creditors waiting in line to be paid, it would likely take years for Enron to clean up the mess that it had made. There was not much chance that anything resembling Enron would remain.

Both in Houston and around the world, many viewed the acts of Kenneth Lay, Jeffrey Skilling, and Andrew Fastow as nothing short of reprehensible. Once bankruptcy was declared and Enron's auditor, Andersen, was accused of being complicit in Enron's accounting deceptions, Enron moved from a financial debacle to a full-fledged scandal. On January 9, 2002, the U.S. Justice Department opened a major criminal investigation to look for wrongdoing at Enron that could lead to federal prosecutions. Attorney General John Ashcroft, who took $57,000 in campaign contributions from Enron and its employees, recused himself from the case under public pressure. The entire Houston office of the Justice Department was also taken off the case because many of them had family or other ties to Enron. Andersen was also being dragged into the case as word of the round-the-clock destruction of Enron-related documents by their Houston office came to light. But soon the focus of the scandal would become an internal memo that would make it less credible for Enron's top executives to plead ignorance.

10

Of Talking Heads and Quiet Deals

On January 14, 2002, a draft of an anonymous seven-page memo to Ken Lay materialized that began with the words: "Has Enron become a risky place to work?" Given that Enron's primary business was the management of risk, this was both provocative and ironic. But the line that the press latched onto appeared later on the front page: "I am incredibly nervous that we will implode in a wave of accounting scandals." To the media, it was now official: Enron had become a scandal.

According to the *Houston Chronicle*, the memo was simply "discovered in a box from Enron headquarters." The next day it was revealed that Sherron Watkins, vice president for corporate development at Enron, had written the memo and sent it anonymously to Ken Lay on August 15, the day after

Jeffrey Skilling resigned. The letter (see the Enron File 1 on p. 185) goes on at length about several of Enron's SPEs, and yet it turns out that Watkins was not privy to the dirtiest details that would later surface. Nonetheless, she saw the potential damage that Jeffrey Skilling's departure would cause Enron: "I believe that the probability of discovery significantly increased with Skilling's shocking departure. Too many people are looking for a smoking gun."

While the leaking of the Watkins memo to the press got

Enron executive and whistle-blower Sherron Watkins testifies as former Enron CEO Jeffrey Skilling watches before the Senate Committee on Commerce, Science and Transportation on February 26, 2002, on Capitol Hill. (© AFP/CORBIS)

the Enron scandal rolling, it was no smoking gun because Watkins, who had recently gone back to work for Andy Fastow, was not in his inner circle. Ken Lay did look into the matter after meeting with Sherron Watkins three times, but he did not follow Watkins' advice to use lawyers and accountants that were not involved in setting up the questionable SPEs. Finally, although her writing the memo was unquestionably an act of bravery, her recommended course of action ("clean up quietly if possible") might be interpreted as a cover-up.

Also on January 14, the world learned about an actual cover-up involving Sherron Watkins' former employer, Andersen. David Duncan, the head of Andersen's Houston office, was fired for ordering the destruction of many Enron-related documents, including some that had been subpoenaed by the SEC. By signing off repeatedly on dubious SPEs, Andersen became part of the Enron scandal. Then, by going the next step to shred documents, it became a ready target for federal prosecutors (see the Enron File 7 on p. 202). Once prosecutors struck a deal with David Duncan, it could go after all of Andersen. Just as Enron could not function with a junk rating for its bonds, Andersen could not function with a felony conviction. With the possibility of a conviction hanging over the firm, Andersen began to unravel. Enron was among the first of Andersen's clients to fire it.

Joseph Berardino, Andersen's chairman, had testified before a joint meeting of the Capital Markets, Insurance, and Government Sponsored Enterprises and the Oversight and Investigations Subcommittees of the House Financial

Services Committee on December 12, 2001, in an effort to defend Andersen. He testified that "it appears important information was not revealed to our team. We've notified the audit committee of possible illegal acts within the company." His defense was that Enron had not told Andersen the truth about its finances and that what it knew had made it suspicious enough to notify Enron's audit committee. Berardino also testified that in the previous year (2000) Andersen had received $52 million in fees from Enron, of which only $25 million could be directly attributed to the audit. Of those fees, $13 million were clearly for consulting work and the remaining $14 million is arguably related to the audit because it is work that can "only be done by auditors," according to Berardino. Because Enron-related revenues were less than 1 percent of Andersen's $9.3 billion annual revenues, Berardino would argue that the money had not corrupted it because it was small relative to the rest of its business. Berardino would resign from his post only after his firm was indicted on criminal charges.

SHREDDED REPUTATION

Enron would soon be accused of a shredding scandal of its own, and pictures of Enron employees who took home boxes of shredded material filled the media. At this point, Ken Lay realized that it was time to call it quits (with the approval of Enron's board of directors and the creditors' committee from its bankruptcy proceeding), so he stepped down as chairman of the board and chief executive officer on January 23. He remained on for a while as a member of Enron's board, but soon even his presence there was no longer constructive.

Enron's inner circle had a tough time ahead of it. In addition to the criminal investigation, the bankruptcy proceedings, and the class-action lawsuits, committees in both the U.S. Senate and House of Representatives were eager to grill Enron executives before a national television audience. Lay, Skilling, Fastow, and others involved in the scandal were hated in their hometown of Houston with an intense Texas hatred. Apparently the ostracism, which Jeff Skilling later compared with that usually reserved for child molesters, got to former Enron vice chairman J. Clifford Baxter, who is believed to have shot himself to death in his own car on January 25. Although the local authorities were quick (some would say too quick) to rule Cliff Baxter's death a suicide, the circumstances surrounding his death were sufficiently suspicious that the case remains open months later. While there is no evidence linking anyone to Baxter's death, given how much Baxter is believed to have known about the inner workings of Enron, his death would seem a bit too convenient. Still, considering the multiple-year ordeal that Baxter would face for his role in the scandal and the pressure to implicate others within the company on criminal charges, his future looked grim.

The month of February would give television viewers a chance to see Enron's inner circle up close, if only to plead the Fifth Amendment. The month began with the release of the 218-page Powers committee report on Enron's SPEs. The Powers committee was formed by Enron's board of directors

Former Enron Corp. vice chairman J. Clifford Baxter in an undated photo. Baxter, 43, was found dead Friday, January 25, 2002, in his Mercedes-Benz, a few miles from his home in Sugar Land, Texas. Authorities believe he died of a self-inflicted gunshot wound to the head. Baxter had resigned from Enron in May 2001, and subsequently became a consultant to Enron. (AP Photo/Texas Department of Public Safety)

at the same time that Fastow was fired from Enron. Its mission was to investigate Fastow's dealings. William Powers, the dean of the University of Texas Law School, led the committee. Powers was recruited as a board member in October to give Enron some credibility. The committee also included Raymond S. Troubh, another new board member, and Herbert S. Winokur Jr. The inclusion of Winokur on the committee cast a shadow over its integrity as he was a board member when many of the deals were approved. It seemed unlikely that the Powers committee would blame Enron's board. Indeed, it generally let board members, including Kenneth Lay, off lightly and reserved its wrath for Andy Fastow, Jeff Skilling, and Andersen's audit work. William Powers resigned from Enron's board two weeks after the report was released.

CLEARER PICTURE

The Powers Report may have been of questionable objectivity when it came to dishing out blame, but it provided an inside look at how Enron's SPEs worked. While the Report itself is a mind-numbing morass of details, William Powers' subsequent testimony before Congress clarified some of the details.

What emerges from the Report is a picture of Enron's slow journey into accounting hell. Andy Fastow, who is painted as the mastermind behind all the SPEs, comes across as a little boy who breaks one rule after another just to see what he can get away with. For his role in those partnerships, Fastow enriched himself by as much as $45 million.

Recall that an important development in Enron's early history was the 1993 Joint Energy Development Investments (JEDI) deal with CalPERS that was legitimately used to purchase power-generating assets without their showing up on Enron's balance sheet. In 1997, Enron wanted to do a similar deal with CalPERS that would be known as JEDI II, but it felt that CalPERS would not be interested unless it could successfully exit the first deal. That is where Chewco, named after Chewbacca, the Wookie from *Star Wars*, enters the picture. Chewco was designed to buy out the CalPERS equity in JEDI I at a hefty profit.

According to the Powers Report, in the process of setting up Chewco, Andy Fastow got away with breaking two rules. First, in order for Enron to keep an SPE off its balance sheet, 3 percent of the equity in the SPE must be held by investors not associated with Enron. Chewco was set up so that it appeared to meet this requirement, but, in fact, it did not. The second problem, according to the Report, was that Andy Fastow's subordinate who ran Chewco, Michael Kopper, never got the required permission from Enron's board of directors. Andy Fastow originally considered running Chewco himself; however, because he was an officer of Enron his position would not only require board approval, it would also have to be publicly disclosed through an SEC filing. If he had Michael Kopper run it, then the public would never know and neither would Enron's board if he (and apparently Jeffrey Skilling as well) never told them. The problem here is that another of Fastow's subordinates was negotiating how much Enron would receive from Chewco for JEDI's assets. The Powers Report posits that Andy Fastow applied pressure to keep Enron from getting the best possible deal. This gave Fastow's man at Chewco a windfall profit and set the stage for even larger profits for Fastow's own SPEs.

CHEWCO STRIKES BACK

In keeping with the *Star Wars* theme, when the Chewco deal closed all the members of the deal team received 18-inch-high fuzzy Chewbacca heads. However, Chewco would strike Enron back. A sizable chunk of the losses that Enron was forced to declare when Ken Lay tried to clean up its books in November 2001 were related to bringing Chewco on board Enron's balance sheet.

The problems with Chewco were straightforward violations of rules that could easily have been remedied without unduly endangering the deal. The Powers committee was unable to determine why Fastow (portrayed as lead villain) felt the need to break the rules. Chewco may well have been a practice run for the first SPE that Fastow would manage. Fastow would depart from the *Star Wars* theme this time and name the new partnership LJM, the initials of his wife, Lea, and his two children. Things were getting personal.

LJM and its much larger successor, LJM2, were set up to fund many deals each. The first LJM deal, known as Rhythms, is a case study in financial chutzpah. While Chewco nibbled around the edges of financial impropriety, Rhythms struck deep at its heart.

While Rhythms was one of Enron's simpler deals, it was also one of its most perverse. A simple analogy for what Fastow did is difficult to conjure up because a good analogy makes sense and Rhythms made no sense.

In March 1998, Enron acquired a $10 million block of shares in Rhythms NetConnections, a high-speed Internet service provider. Enron was not allowed to sell these shares until the end of 1999. In April 1999, Rhythms went public and its stock soared to where Enron's investment was now worth $300 million. Enron's accounting rules required it to mark the shares to market every day. This meant that Enron had already booked $290 million of profits on the transaction, but it was concerned that going forward it might have to book substantial losses. Because it could not sell the shares for several months, it wanted to get insurance against a significant decline in Rhythms shares. The standard way for investors to acquire such insurance is through the purchase of a put option. A put option locks in a specific sale price for the shares for the life of the option. For example, with Rhythms trading at $65 per share, Enron might want to purchase a put option good until the end of the year that locks in a price of $60. This option would not cover the first $5 of loss (you can think of that as the deductible on the insurance policy), but covers the rest of the loss dollar for dollar. As with any other type of insurance policy, the smaller the deductible, the more the insurance costs.

Enron's problem was that its block of Rhythms shares was so large and the company was so risky that there was no one on Wall Street willing to provide this insurance at what Enron considered a reasonable price. According to the Report, Fastow's solution was to create a company that he would run that used Enron stock as its capital to sell the insurance on Rhythms stock to Enron. If the insurance was never needed, Fastow and his partners, who were chosen from his subordinates at Enron, could pocket much of the premium that Enron paid and become quite rich. If Rhythms stock plummeted, the Enron stock that backed their company would bail them out. The big problem was that if both Rhythms and Enron stock fell far enough, the company would go broke unless someone (Enron) bailed it out. Because Enron was essentially insuring itself, with Fastow and his associates taking large fees in the process, there really wasn't any insurance.

It is wild enough that Fastow appears to have thought up this scheme. What is even wilder is that it got past Enron's board, Andersen's auditor, and Enron's law firm, Vinson & Elkins. The Powers Report indicates that what Enron's board approved and what Fastow did were two very different things. Enron's board did approve a waiver of its Code of Conduct to allow Fastow to set up LJM, the SPE that did the Rhythms deal. Andersen would later admit to errors of a technical nature—like Chewco, this deal also lacked sufficient outside equity and Andersen failed to notice—but nothing more.

RAPTORS

The sequel to LJM, called LJM2, represented the final step in Fastow's evolution of the SPE. According to the Report, the major deals that went into LJM2 were the four Raptors, a name inspired by the dinosaurs in the movie *Jurassic Park*. The Raptors were modeled after the Rhythms deal but were far more complex. While Rhythms was designed to provide a faulty hedge against a profitable investment, the Raptors were used to bury the losses of unprofitable ones. In total, the Raptors were used to hide $1.1 billion in Enron losses. Sherron Watkins' memo to Kenneth Lay was precipitated by what she had heard about the Raptors.

With the Powers Report released, the Congressional

investigations as well as the media circus that surrounded them could begin in earnest. Earlier hearings the previous December were limited to those with peripheral involvement in the scandal. The Fifth Amendment, however, posed a major problem for the dozen or so Congressmen at hearings wishing to question top Enron executives. Those with any prospect of facing either civil or criminal proceedings could have this testimony used as evidence against them. The Fifth Amendment gives individuals the right not to incriminate themselves even when testifying before Congress unless they are granted immunity. Congress saw no reason to grant immunity to anyone involved in the Enron scandal. While it may create the appearance of guilt to plead the Fifth before a Congressional committee, the lawyers interviewed by the media virtually all seemed to agree that for the big players at Enron—Lay, Skilling, and Fastow—to do so was the only prudent course.

Before the February hearings began, word had it that Lay and Skilling would testify regardless of the legal jeopardy that might result and that Fastow had fled the country. Skilling did testify, but Lay and Fastow would not. Fastow was still in the United States and would take the Fifth. Lay had agreed to testify in early January, but an odd chain of events would cause him to change his mind.

Ken Lay's wife, Linda Lay, was interviewed by Lisa Myers of the *Today* show just days before the Powers Report was released. While most of the January 28 interview has Linda giving a touching, tearful defense of her husband as a decent and honest man, the following exchange attracted all of the media attention:

LISA MYERS: According to published reports, your husband earned about $300 million in compensation and stock from Enron over the last four years. What happened to all that money?

LINDA LAY: By anyone's standards, it was a massive amount of money, and it's gone. It's gone. There's nothing left. Everything we had mostly was in Enron stock. I mean, it was him. Ken built the company. We believed in it. It was a good stock.

HOLLOW WORDS

In light of the massive losses inflicted on Enron's employees, Linda Lay's appeal for sympathy by claiming "there's nothing left" rang hollow and created an enormous backlash against her and her husband. Late-night comedians, newspaper columnists, and pundits of all stripes had a field day with the comment. (A few months after the interview Linda Lay would open a store in Houston called Jus' Stuff to sell some of the family belongings to raise cash.)

A day or so after the Linda Lay interview, a tape from an October 2001 Enron employee meeting would surface that would provide further fodder for comedians. As is typical of such meetings, Ken Lay solicited written questions from the employees. Here is one of the questions that he read aloud to those in attendance:

> I would like to know if you are on crack. If so, that would explain a lot. If not, maybe you ought to start because it is going to be a long time before we trust you again.

On February 3, the night before Ken Lay was scheduled to testify before the Senate Commerce, Science and Transportation Committee, his lawyer, Earl J. Silbert, sent a letter to the committee's chairman, Senator Ernest Hollings, indicating that Lay would no longer testify (see the Enron File 10 on p. 207). Silbert saw the tone of the committee as being "prosecutorial" and presented as evidence several quotes taken from televised interviews with members of the Commerce Committee and others in Congress. Sherron Watkins would ultimately assume the role of Ken Lay's defender at the hearings.

Lacking its star witness, the Senate Commerce Committee regrouped, and the House Energy and Commerce Committee began its own hearings on February 5. The first day of hearings was spent quizzing William Powers about his committee's report. The hearings were chaired by Louisiana Republican Representative W. J. "Billy" Tauzin who, like many other members of the committee, had received campaign contributions from some of the Enron executives who would be appearing before his committee. (See Figure 10.1 for a summary of Enron's contributions to Congress.) Some network feeds of the hearings flashed a summary of the Enron contributions that each committee member had received every time he or she appeared on camera. (The networks did not show either how much they themselves had contributed to each member or how much advertising money they had received from Enron.)

After a number of academic and industry experts made presentations to the committee on February 6, the real fireworks began on February 7. The proceedings that day would be divided into three acts. Act I saw Andrew Fastow, Michael

Enron's Total Lobbying Expenditures (1997–2000)

1997	$1.080 million
1998	$1.600 million
1999	$1.940 million
2000	$2.030 million

Top Congressional Recipients of Enron Contributions (1989–2001)*

Senate	
Democrats (29 members)	$110,513
Republicans (41 members)	$417,480
House	
Democrats (71 members)	$257,140
Republicans (117 members)	$346,348

Largest Enron Contributions to Members of U.S. Senate and House of Representatives (1989–2001)*

Senate	
Kay Bailey Hutchinson (R-Texas)	$99,500
Phil Gramm (R-Texas)	$97,350
Conrad Burns (R-Montana)	$23,200
Charles E. Schumer (D-New York)	$21,933
Michael D. Crapo (R-Idaho)	$18,689
Christopher S. Bond (R-Missouri)	$18,500
Gordon Smith (R-Oregon)	$18,000
Jeff Bingaman (D-New Mexico)	$14,124
Chuck Hagel (R-Nebraska)	$13,331
Pete V. Domenici (R-New Mexico)	$12,000
John B. Breaux (D-Lousiana)	$11,100
John McCain (R-Arizona)	$9,500
House	
Ken Bentsen (R-Texas)	$42,750
Sheila Jackson Lee (D-Texas)	$38,000
Joe L. Barton (R-Texas)	$28,909
Tom DeLay (R-Texas)	$28,900
Martin Frost (D-Texas)	$24,250
Charles W. Stenholm (D-Texas)	$14,439
Chet Edwards (D-Texas)	$10,000
Doug Bereuter (R-Nebraska)	$10,000
Larry Combest (R-Texas)	$9,820
John D. Dingell (D-Michigan)	$9,000
Edward J. Markey (D-Massachusetts)	$8,500
Earl Blumenauer (D-Oregon)	$8,000

*Based on Federal Election Commission (FEC) data on 11/1/01. Total contributions from Enron's political action committee (PAC) and its employees. Totals do not reflect contributions recently returned.
Source: The Center for Responsive Politics.

Figure 10.1 **Enron's Contributions to Congress**

Kopper, and two Enron staff members take the Fifth. This involved the sort of public humiliation that Cliff Baxter had likely wished to avoid. Enron executives would not simply be allowed to take the Fifth Amendment and leave. As punishment, they had to sit before the committee as member after member would denounce their actions in what might be viewed as an effort to goad them to speak up in their own defense. None of them did.

Act II centered on making the case against Andrew Fastow and Jeffrey Skilling. First up from Enron was Jeffrey McMahon, who had worked for Andy Fastow but was not among his inner circle. McMahon took over from Fastow when he was fired and then was promoted to be the president and chief operating officer of Enron. McMahon testified that he saw Fastow's participation in the SPEs as a conflict of interest and went to Jeffrey Skilling to complain about the situation (see the Enron Files 4 and 5 on pp. 198 and 199). At the time of this complaint, McMahon was Enron's treasurer and had the job of negotiating on Enron's behalf with some of Fastow's other subordinates. He told Skilling of how this put him in a bind. Shortly after that meeting, McMahon was transferred to a position that he saw as a demotion. Enron lawyer Jordan Mintz detailed his frustrations in dealing with Skilling. He was unable to get Skilling to see any problem with Fastow's arguable conflicts of interest and could not get Skilling to sign off on deal approval forms that Mintz believed required Skilling's signature (see the Enron File 3 on p. 195). A few deals got through without Skilling's signature and there was no satisfactory explanation for how this could have occurred.

After a lunch break, Act III began with the much-awaited appearance of Jeffrey Skilling. He would contradict the morning testimony of McMahon and Mintz. He recalled the McMahon meeting as being about general job dissatisfaction—McMahon's move was supposed to be a promotion—and argued that none of the deals required his approval. In general, he denied knowing anything at all about Andy Fastow's dealings. Committee members repeatedly informed him that he was supposed to be smart and have a great mind for details, to which Skilling unwaveringly responded, "I am not an accountant." The most bizarre part of Skilling's testimony came when he was confronted with the fact that he was recorded as present at a meeting in a West Palm Beach, Florida, hotel where the Fastow deals were discussed. In response, Skilling elaborately explained how the power in the hotel went out and how people were coming in and out of the room without being seen. Apparently he may have been in the men's room or on a cell phone at the time of the Fastow discussion and not in the darkened meeting room.

In the course of the afternoon, Skilling did present his view as to what went wrong at Enron. In his opening statement he said (and would later repeat):

> [I]t is my belief that Enron's failure was due to a classic "run on the bank": a liquidity crisis spurred by a lack of confidence in the company. At the time of Enron's collapse, the company was solvent and highly profitable—but, apparently, not liquid enough.

As we saw earlier, the expectation that Enron would lose its investment-grade credit rating did indeed undermine its business. Ultimately, even the newly promoted McMahon would resign from Enron as it attempted to emerge from bankruptcy. Given the repeated restatements of Enron's financial results, however, Enron was not even profitable, much less highly profitable. With more debt surfacing on its balance sheet every day, its solvency was questionable. (A company is solvent if the value of its assets exceeds the claims against those assets—in other words, if it were forced to sell everything and pay off its debts, it would still have something left over.)

The senators expressed disbelief at what Skilling told them and would bring in Sherron Watkins a week later to further contradict him. The committee built Watkins up as the hero of the whole affair, and Michigan Republican John Dingell called her "an extraordinary, courageous woman, who has been a bright spot in an otherwise sorry and outrageous saga." Watkins looked the part of an honest, concerned employee. The only things that kept her from being canonized on the spot by the committee were that she never got up the nerve to directly confront either Jeffrey Skilling or Andrew Fastow (which would lead Jeffrey Skilling's lawyer, Bruce Hiler, to say, "Everything Ms. Watkins said about my client is based on hearsay, rumor, or her opinion") and that she was a staunch defender of Ken Lay. Watkins claimed that Lay had been "duped" by Skilling and Fastow. One of the exhibits presented to the committee is an October 30, 2001, e-mail from Watkins to Enron's public relations department that can be viewed as a list of "talking points." (See the Enron File 2 on p. 192.) Among other things, the memo advised Lay to say that he relied on Skilling and Fastow "to manage the details" and "he trusted the wrong people."

FAMOUS LAST WORDS

In the meantime, after attempts to get Kenneth Lay to change his mind and testify before the Senate Commerce Committee failed, he was brought before them on February 12 to endure an hour of hazing before pleading the Fifth. Undoubtedly aware that they were being upstaged by the House Energy and Commerce Committee, the Senate Commerce Committee arranged a February 26 hearing that would place Jeffrey Skilling in the same room with Sherron Watkins and Jeffrey McMahon, hoping to see Skilling squirm. This session turned up little that was new. Sherron Watkins still felt that Kenneth Lay had been duped, but also blamed him for failing to respond properly to her concerns and was "disappointed" with his actions. Furthermore, at one point Watkins even agreed with Skilling on a major point by saying, "I think Mr. Skilling is correct that what killed the company was a run on the bank."

Skilling began with an opening statement in which he appeared to be lecturing the senators. He reminded them that "The framers of the Bill of Rights are watching" and with anger in his voice said, "Unfortunately, neither common decency nor common sense will carry the day in *this* politicized process." He, like whatever viewers were left watching the hearings, had observed the tendency for members of Congress to be more concerned with making speeches to the television cameras than they were with learning about Enron. In both his opening statement and in the proceedings that followed he would restate what now must have been his mantra, "I am not an accountant."

11

The Only Place to End the Enron Story

The Enron story has only just begun now that the company and we are here in Chapter 11. There are dozens of pending lawsuits against the company and those who ran it. Jeffrey Skilling estimated during his Senate Commerce Committee testimony that he was already named in 36 suits, and more have subsequently been filed. Potential criminal charges are not out of the question. Further twists and turns in the story are almost inevitable, and many of the mysteries may never be solved. How much did Kenneth Lay and Jeffrey Skilling know about Fastow's deals? How did Fastow think them up and why did he think he could get away with them? What were the circumstances behind Cliff Baxter's death? What role in the failure should be assigned to others at Enron?

Investors, seeing what happened to Enron, had their own questions. How many other Enrons were out there? Can any company's financial statements be trusted? Might the federal government itself be one gigantic Enron? A new ailment called Enronitis began to infect the stock market. Enron's competitors and large companies like Tyco, General Electric, and IBM all faced hard questions in the wake of the Enron disaster. These companies had financial statements that appeared to hide more than they revealed, and they saw their stocks drop precipitously as investors abandoned them. Faced with a market reaction that they could not ignore, many companies made additional disclosures to investors, but the market clearly wanted more.

What Enron did was to take the standard practices that most companies use to put the best face on their finances and stretched those practices to an extreme that created the appearance of fraud. (The courts will decide whether it was fraud.) As accounting firms have grown from stodgy partnerships to international consulting behemoths whose top partners make millions of dollars a year, their ability to enforce strict accounting standards has been called into question.

While minor manipulations of corporate finances may be common (and still need to be cleaned up), what Enron did was so extreme that it will likely dwarf any similar problems. The company's remote location in Houston rather than in one of the country's traditional financial centers—rather than New York, Chicago, Boston, or San Francisco—may have contributed to its problems. In a financial center, there is a strong sense of community among its workers. A typical career path involves several moves from company to company, and productive workers unhappy with their present employers can usually find other jobs without uprooting their families. Social norms are developed because everyone knows how a financial firm is supposed to operate. They learn what behavior is proper and what is improper. This does not mean improprieties cannot happen, just that when they do they are likely to be more limited than what happened at Enron.

Enron had developed as an island in the world of finance. While some of Enron's people came from the outside, Enron preferred to recruit its employees straight out of school so that they would know only the Enron way of doing things. Workers who had risen through the ranks at Enron and put down roots in Houston would have difficulty finding a similar job in Houston with similar pay. Facing limited alternatives, people would find it easier to tolerate or ignore the sinister things that were going on at Enron. It was clear to those who worked at Enron that they were in a unique situation and hopefully Enron's problems were unique. Still, Wall Street has had its share of financial scandals in the past and, given the money at stake, can be counted on to have more in the future.

STOPPING THE NEXT ENRON

Now that we have seen one Enron, what can be done to prevent more? This is a question with no simple answers.

The accounting profession is trying to respond to the "crisis in accounting" brought on by the Enron affair, but radical changes in self-governance have been ruled out. The remaining international accounting giants are reluctant to part with their lucrative consulting practices or change the policy of having the company being audited (rather than the stock exchange or some government agency) pay for the audit.

In a case like Enron's, business schools seem to be the natural target. Previous scandals have led to the requirement that business schools include business ethics in their curricula in order to be accredited. Ethics was not a part of Harvard Business School's curriculum when Jeffrey Skilling was there, and the situation is not much better today. Many students are believed to view ethics as being about not getting caught rather than how to do the right thing in the first place.

The economic foundation upon which the financial markets operate lies outside the context of ethics and morals. In an ideal market system—such as formed the basis for the theories of Long-Term Capital Management's financial gurus, Robert Merton and Myron Scholes—individuals pursuing their own best interests will end up serving the collective good. While the decline of socialism has shown that the basic idea behind leaving most economic decision making to the market mechanism is sound, markets do not work perfectly, as Merton and Scholes would learn the hard way through the collapse of LTCM.

The traditional view of markets assumes that while self-interest will determine what people choose, they will not choose to break the rules of the market. While common thievery is clearly a violation of market rules, so is the financial fiddling that Enron acknowledged when it restated its profits in October 2001. While a certain amount of "crime and punishment" can be built into an economic system, there is a growing school of economic thought that markets can function effectively only in societies where most people are honest. By the time someone gets to business school, it is already too late to teach the proper values.

Conservatives and liberals may disagree as to how much control the government should exert over businesses, but they tend to agree that businesses cannot function properly in an unethical and amoral environment. The study of economics and its application to the financial markets is moving away from treating individuals and businesses merely as if they were pleasure-seeking computers.

SOCIAL CAPITAL

Economists, political scientists, and sociologists have been working together on the importance of "social capital" to the functioning of modern economics. Social capital can be viewed as the web of connections that link people together, such as family, religious, civic, and social action groups. An economy with a good stock of social capital is believed to be better able to follow the rules required to make any economic system function well. Governments, no matter how good their intentions, should take into account the effect their actions have on the stock of social capital.

Other economists are working with psychologists and

biologists to examine how people really behave in market situations and how the knowledge of this behavior can be used to make markets work better. There is strong evidence, much of it gained from markets created in a controlled environment, that the assumptions upon which the financial markets have been constructed are flawed. Furthermore, these flaws may account for what some see as the excess volatility of the financial markets.

While markets and the individuals who transact in them may not be perfect, the financial markets' reaction to the Enron scandal has shown how powerful markets can be. While Jeffrey Skilling and Sherron Watkins saw the market as unduly punishing Enron by a "run on the bank," that was the market's way of enforcing its standards for honesty on Enron. Other companies, fearing the wrath of the market, were immediately forced to be more forthcoming without any deliberative action from the accounting profession or the government. The true lesson of Enron is that one who lives by the market can also die by the market.

Cast of Characters

The following is a guide to the people involved in the Enron debacle, complete with background information. Not all people listed have been covered by us in the book, but they have been featured in the news at some point. For those who want to know who is who and follow the news, the following "credits" should be helpful.

STARRING . . .

Kenneth Lay, former chairman and chief executive officer, Enron. Kenneth Lay was born on April 15, 1942, in Tyrone, Missouri. He grew up in rural Missouri and received his bachelor's and master's degrees in economics from the University of Missouri. His career in the energy business began in 1965 when he joined what is now ExxonMobil as a corporate economist in Houston, Texas. While working there and at subsequent jobs, he completed a Ph.D. in economics at the University of Houston.

Kenneth Lay spent several years in Washington, D.C. He was a naval officer and worked on energy policy for the federal government at the Federal Energy Regulatory Commission and the U.S. Department of the Interior. Lay was also an assistant professor at George Washington University.

Lay returned to the private sector and ultimately became president of Florida Gas Company (now Continental Resources Company). He then moved to Transco Energy Company as its president and chief operating officer. In June 1984, he left Transco to become chairman and chief executive officer of Houston Natural Gas. After the acquisition of Houston Natural Gas by InterNorth, Inc., Lay would become its chairman and chief executive officer in July 1985 and the company would be renamed Enron in February 1986. He stepped down as chief executive officer in February 2001, but reassumed the position with the departure of Jeffrey Skilling in August 2001. In January 2002, Lay would resign as both chairman and chief executive officer and the following month vacate his seat on the board of directors.

While he was head of Enron, Lay was known for philanthropic work, especially in the Houston area. He also contributed heavily to political campaigns and political action committees for both Republican and Democratic candidates both locally and nationally.

Jeffrey Skilling, former chief executive officer of Enron, was born on November 25, 1953, in Pittsburgh, Pennsylvania. He worked as a teenager along with his brother Thomas, who would later become a Chicago television weatherman, at an Aurora, Illinois, television station as its chief production director. Growing up, Skilling was physically active and broke several bones, including some in his back, during a variety of endeavors.

Skilling received his bachelor's degree in applied science from Southern Methodist University. He then went to work as a corporate planning officer with First City National Bank of Houston before going on to receive a master's in business administration from Harvard Business School, where he graduated as a Baker Scholar in 1979.

From business school, Skilling joined McKinsey & Company, where he became a senior partner. After an extended consulting engagement with Enron, he joined the company in 1990 to head up its trading business. He was named president and chief operating officer of Enron in December 1996 and would rise to chief executive officer in February 2001. He unexpectedly resigned "for personal reasons" in August 2001.

Skilling is generally considered the master strategist behind Enron's transformation from a traditional natural gas pipeline operator to a new-economy trading company. He is described as a detail-obsessed manager who carefully engineered Enron's rise to prominence. In testimony that he provided House and Senate committees in February 2002 he said he was unaware of the details or of any improprieties behind the SPEs that Enron had set up to inflate its earnings and hide its debt.

Andrew Fastow, former chief financial officer of Enron, was born December 22, 1961, in Washington, D.C. He grew up in suburban New Jersey and attended Tufts University where he met his future wife, Lea Weingarten, whose father owned a large chain of supermarkets and a real estate firm in the Houston area. He graduated from Tufts with a bachelor's degree in economics and Chinese and then received a master's in business administration from Northwestern University. Upon graduation in 1986, he joined Continental Bank Corp. in Chicago where he would become the bank's expert in asset securitization. Enron Capital, an Enron subsidiary, hired Fastow in 1990. There he met and became friends with Jeffrey Skilling. In 1996, he headed Enron's push into retail electricity markets and became chief financial officer of Enron in 1998 at the age of 37, considered young for someone taking the top financial post at a major corporation.

As Enron's chief financial officer, Fastow used his background in asset securitization to develop new types of special purpose entities (SPEs) for Enron. Fastow's participation in these SPEs along with questions about their legitimacy led to his resignation from Enron in October 2001. Fastow has not spoken publicly about his role in Enron's collapse and has declined to testify before Congressional committees that are looking into it.

Sherron Watkins was a relatively obscure vice president of corporate development at Enron until the world learned of her memo to Kenneth Lay in January 2002. A second cousin of Texas country music singer Lyle Lovett, Watkins studied accounting at the University of Texas where she received both bachelor's and master's degrees.

In 1982, she joined the accounting firm of Arthur Andersen (now Andersen), working first in Houston and then in New York. She left in 1990 to work in New York for Metallgesellschaft, a company that had serious financial problems in 1993, the year that Watkins left to work for Andrew Fastow at Enron. She was brought to Houston to manage Fastow's first major SPE, known as JEDI. She would work at various jobs in Enron before coming back to work for Fastow, who was now chief financial officer, in June 2001.

Watkins' job in Fastow's group was to find assets that Enron might sell to raise cash. While doing this work, she noticed irregularities in the Raptor transactions that in the wake of Jeffrey Skilling's departure led her to write a memo expressing her concerns to Kenneth Lay. Shortly after writing the memo, she was transferred out of Fastow's group and into the human resources group. The discovery of these irregularities by the financial markets was instrumental in precipitating Enron's downfall. Even after Enron declared bankruptcy and she testified before Congress about her efforts to get Enron to rectify its accounts, Watkins continued to work for Enron.

John Clifford ("Cliff") Baxter was born in 1958 in Amityville, New York. He went to New York University for his undergraduate studies and then joined the U.S. Air Force where he served as a captain from 1980 to 1985. He then went to Columbia Business School where he received a master's in business administration in 1987. Baxter worked as an investment banker before joining Enron in 1991. He had several high management positions in the firm before becoming vice chairman in October 2000. He resigned several months later, in May 2001, to "spend additional time with his family," according to the Enron press release. While at Enron, Baxter is reported to have been upset about Andrew Fastow's LJM transactions and is said to have complained bitterly to Jeffrey Skilling about them.

Cliff Baxter's departure was noticed only by those who knew and respected him within Enron. The business press largely ignored him until he was discovered dead of a gunshot wound in his car along a median strip not far from his Sugar Land, Texas, home in the early hours of January 25, 2002. Although initially considered a suicide, the circumstances of his death, including a block-lettered suicide note without a signature and other details surrounding his death, have raised suspicions.

Rebecca Mark was chief executive officer of Azurix, an Enron spin-off that sought to develop water markets on a global scale. She attended Baylor University where she received a master's in international management in 1977. She worked at First City National Bank in Houston before joining one of Enron's predecessor companies. She worked for a power business at Enron that was partially sold to Dominion Resources in 1987. She continued part-time at Enron for the next two years while getting a master's in business administration at Harvard Business School. In 1991, she became chairman and chief executive officer of Enron Development Corp., a group at Enron that acquired international assets for the company. In this position Mark became a legend. Her aggressiveness as a negotiator earned her the nickname "Mark the Shark" as she relentlessly jetted around the world making deals for Enron. Her most famous deal was the Dabhol power project in India, which she rescued from oblivion in 1996. She was named vice chairman of Enron in 1998.

In 1998, *Business 2.0* magazine named Mark the 14th most powerful woman in corporate America (just three slots below Martha Stewart), and she has received similar honors from other business publications including *Fortune*. She started Azurix in 1999, but after an unsuccessful initial public offering and several business setbacks, she resigned in August 2000. Many of the assets that she acquired for Enron, including the Dabhol power project, would fail to deliver the profits that had motivated their acquisition.

IN A SUPPORTING ROLE . . .

Ray Bowen is currently Executive Vice President and Chief Financial Officer of the postbankruptcy Enron.

Richard B. Buy was formerly executive vice president and chief risk officer. Terminated by Enron on February 14, 2002, after release of the Powers Report.

Richard A. Causey was formerly executive vice president and chief accounting officer. Terminated by Enron on February 14, 2002, after release of the Powers Report.

Stephen Cooper serves as acting Chief Executive Officer and Chief Restructuring Officer of postbankruptcy Enron.

James V. Derrick Jr. was executive vice president and general counsel. Served Enron since June 1991. Retired on March 1, 2002.

Mark A. Frevert was promoted to vice chairman on August 28, 2001, to shore up Enron's management team. Joined Lay and Whalley as part of Enron's Office of the Chairman after Skilling's resignation on August 14, 2001. Now part of UBS Warburg acquisition of Enron's trading operations.

Ben Glisan was former treasurer at Enron. An accountant who later became McMahon's successor as treasurer. Was a participant in two transactions that ultimately required restatements of earnings and equity: Chewco and the Raptor structures. Reportedly cooperating with the Justice Department's investigation.

Michael J. Kopper was managing director in Enron Global Finance. A low-profile character who earned millions through structuring and participating in Enron suspect partnerships with Andrew Fastow.

Jeff McMahon was president and chief operating officer of postbankruptcy Enron before resigning on April 19, 2002, due to pressures from credit agencies. McMahon was Enron's treasurer during Skilling's tenure as CEO, and later was shuffled by Skilling into a position as chairman and CEO of Enron's Industrial Markets.

Lou Pai was former president and chief operating officer of Enron Capital and Trade Resources. In March 1997 named chairman of Enron Energy Services (EES), a separate operating company at Enron serving retail gas and electricity markets as they opened to competition.

William C. Powers Jr. is dean of University of Texas School of Law. Joined Enron board on October 31, 2001, for purpose of chairing the Special Investigation Committee. After completing the Powers Report, resigned from Enron board on February 14, 2002.

Joseph W. Sutton was vice chairman of Enron in July 1999. Joined Ken Lay and Jeff Skilling in Office of the Chairman at that time. Prior to that position, was chairman and CEO of Enron International. Left Enron in November 2000.

Lawrence G. Whalley was president and chief operating officer of Enron Corp. for short time. Accepted a position with UBS Warburg as part of UBS buyout transaction with Enron. Joined Lay in Enron's Office of the Chairman on August 28, 2001, along with Mark Frevert, after Skilling's resignation.

Thomas White was vice chairman of Enron Energy Services from 1998 to May 2001. Appointed by President George W. Bush to be Secretary of the Army and still embroiled in Enron controversy.

AND ALSO . . .

Maureen Castaneda is a former Enron executive who claims the shredding of documents on Enron's premises began after Thanksgiving at Houston headquarters.

David Duncan was Andersen's chief auditor on Enron account until he was fired January 14, 2002.

Nancy Temple is a lawyer for Andersen who reiterated the firm's document-destruction policy in an October 12 e-mail to its Houston office.

Chuck Watson was Chairman and CEO, Dynegy. Resigned on May 28, 2002.

Enron Board of Directors (before Bankruptcy)

Robert A. Belfer
Norman P. Blake Jr.
Ronnie C. Chan
John H. Duncan
Wendy L. Gramm
Robert K. Jaedicke
Charles A. Lemaistre
John Mendelsohn
Paulo V. Ferraz Pereira
William C. Powers Jr.
Frank Savage
John Wakeham
Herbert S. Winokur Jr.

Enron's Current Board of Directors

Robert A. Belfer
Norman P. Blake Jr.
Wendy L. Gramm
John Mendelsohn
Frank Savage
Raymond S. Troubh
Herbert S. Winokur Jr.

Through the Pipeline: An Enron Time Line

1980s

New regulations gradually create a market-pricing system for natural gas. Federal Energy Regulatory Commission (FERC) Order 436 (1985) provides blanket approval for pipelines that choose to become common carriers transporting gas intrastate, FERC Order 451 (1986) deregulates the wellhead, and FERC Order 490 (April 1988) authorizes producers, pipelines, and others to terminate gas sales or purchases without seeking prior FERC approval. As a result of these orders, more than 75 percent of gas sales are conducted through the spot market, and unprecedented market volatility exists. Both short- and long-term risk transfer products as well as reliable gas delivery at both fixed and floating prices are needed.

This time line comes from multiple sources, including the authors' own firsthand experiences and research, and "Enron Milestones," a time line on Enron Corp.'s company web site. The secondary sources include time lines and dates from the *Houston Chronicle*, *Washington Post*, *U.S. News & World Report*, BBC, *Financial Times*, Global Change Associates, and the Powers Report.

1984 Ken Lay is chairman and CEO of Houston Natural Gas.

1985 Lay engineers merger between Houston Natural Gas and InterNorth, a natural gas pipeline company.

Lay is named chairman of new company after boardroom coup.

Richard Kinder, who later becomes Lay's number two man as the company's president and chief operating officer, connects with Lay from the start.

1986 Company changes name to Enron and moves headquarters to Houston, where Lay lives. Enron is both a natural gas and an oil company.

1987 Enron Oil, Enron's flourishing petroleum marketing operation, reports loss of $85 million in 8-K filings. True loss of $142 to $190 million is concealed until 1993. Two top Enron Oil executives plead guilty to conspiracy to defraud and to filing false tax returns. One serves time in prison.

1988 As deregulation of natural gas market continues, Enron shifts business strategy to be both physical supplier of natural gas and a "gas bank" offering financing and risk management services to the energy industry.

Enron enters U.K. energy market. Becomes first U.S. company to construct power plant (Teeside) in Britain after electric industry there is privatized.

1989 Enron launches GasBank, allowing natural gas producers and wholesale buyers to purchase gas supplies at set prices while hedging price swings using customized physical contracts and financially settled derivatives contracts.

Enron begins offering financing to oil and gas producers.

Transwestern Pipeline Company, owned by Enron, is the first merchant pipeline in the United States to stop selling gas and become a transportation-only pipeline.

1990 Enron launches plan to expand U.S. natural gas business abroad.

Enron becomes a natural-gas market maker in the United States. Begins trading futures and options on the New York Mercantile Exchange and over-the-counter market using financial instruments such as swaps and options.

Lay and Kinder hire Jeffrey Skilling from McKinsey & Company to become chief executive officer of Enron Gas Services, Enron's "gas bank." Enron Gas Services mutates ultimately into Enron Capital and Trade Resources (ECT).

Skilling hires Andrew Fastow from the banking industry; he starts as account director and quickly rises within the ranks of ECT.

1991 Tearing a page from Wall Street's playbook, Enron adopts mark-to-market accounting practices, reporting income and value of assets at their replacement cost.

Enron's Fastow forms the first of many off-balance-sheet partnerships for legitimate business purposes. Later in Enron's history, off-balance-sheet partnerships and transactions will become a way for money-losing ventures to be concealed and income reporting to be accelerated.

1992 Enron acquires Transportadora de Gas del Sur. Starts rolling out "energy network" concept around the world, which includes natural gas pipelines, electric and natural gas utilities, and wholesale commodities trading and energy services.

Government continues deregulating, allowing Enron to create distinct businesses for the transportation and selling of gas. Opens door for Enron market maker in energy and power, bundling physical delivery with risk management services.

1993 Wendy Gramm, former chair of the federal agency that regulates energy trading, joins Enron's board. During her tenure at the Commodity Futures Trading Commission (CFTC), energy swaps have become exempt from CFTC oversight, paving the way for Enron's aggressive entry in over-the-counter derivative markets.

Enron's Teeside power plant in Britain begins operation. Becomes world's largest gas-fired heat and power facility.

Enron and the California Public Employees' Retirement System (CalPERS) form the Joint Energy Development Investments (JEDI) limited partnerships. CalPERS is one of the largest pension plans in the world. JEDI is formed to invest in natural gas projects.

1994 Enron begins trading electricity in the United States as power market deregulation intensifies. Enron soon will become the largest U.S. marketer of electricity.

1995 Enron establishes a trading center in London and begins trading power and gas in Britain. Enron soon will become the largest merchant of natural gas and power in Britain and a major presence in all of Europe.

1996 Regulatory barrier in United States removed for wholesale power transmission of electricity.

Spearheaded by Rebecca Mark, cochair and CEO of Enron Operations Corp. who later became chairman and CEO of Enron International in January 1997, Enron begins construction of $2 billion Dabhol power plant in India with General Electric and Bechtel. Becomes first power project in India to involve imported liquefied natural gas.

Richard Kinder resigns as president and COO of Enron to start his own company.

Lay, chairman and CEO of Enron since 1986, names Jeffrey Skilling Enron's president and chief operating officer, replacing Kinder. Skilling continues as president of Enron Capital and Trade Resources, one of the most profitable and powerful units within Enron.

1997 Enron begins construction of another major power station in Britain at Sutton Bridge.

Enron announces the settlement of all contractual issues involving the J-block contract, a major supply deal, in Britain. Enron records a second-quarter nonrecurring charge to income of $450 million after tax.

Enron extends energy-trading model to new commodities markets. Begins trading weather derivative products and looks to develop markets in coal, pulp and paper, plastics, metals, and bandwidth capacity.

Enron Energy Services (EES) is launched, with Lou Pai named chief executive officer, to bundle wholesale energy delivery and risk management services to commercial and industrial users. EES will do its first deal with General Cable in 1998 and sign up contracts of nearly $209 billion in two years.

Enron's Northern Natural Gas pipeline initiates a major marketwide expansion project to be completed in five years. It will increase the pipeline's contract capacity by 350,000 million cubic feet of gas per day.

Enron interested in buying out CalPERS' stake in JEDI partnership so it can persuade CalPERS to participate in larger partnership deal.

Enron creates Chewco to purchase CalPERS' stake in JEDI but keep partnership off balance sheet. Enron seeks to keep Chewco off its balance sheet by granting it independent ownership status, but ultimately does not satisfy the 3 percent equity hurdle required to do so. Nevertheless, Chewco remains off balance sheet.

1998 Enron invests $10 million in Rhythms NetConnections, Inc., a privately held Internet service provider for businesses that uses digital subscriber technology.

Rhythms goes public at $21 per share but reaches $69 by the close of its first trading day. Enron's $10 million investment will be worth $300 million in a year.

Enron buys Wessex Water in Britain and forms Azurix, a water utility company. Rebecca Mark becomes CEO of new company.

Spain and Germany award Enron the first power marketing licenses granted to new market participants following the passage of national electricity regulations.

Enron's Northern Border Pipeline in the United States completes its third and most ambitious expansion. Project involves 390 miles of gas pipelines running from Iowa to Illinois.

1999 New Houston Astros baseball stadium is named Enron Field. Enron Energy Services is awarded 30-year contract to ballpark with energy management services.

Enron forms Enron Broadband Services (EBS) to invest in broadband market and to trade bandwidth capacity.

EBS launches Enron Intelligent Network (EIN), an Internet application delivery platform.

Enron's Dabhol power plant in India becomes world's largest independent natural-gas-fired power facility. But it remains troubled under a legal cloud and experiences poor operating results.

EnronOnline is launched, a business-to-business Internet platform designed to trade commodities. Within two years, the platform will average 6,000 trades per day worth $2.5 billion and become the world's largest business-to-business trading platform.

Azurix, Enron's water company, goes public in an IPO.

Enron's board of directors appoints CFO Fastow general partner of two LJM partnerships, which requires special approval due to possible conflict of interest in serving this dual role. Ultimately, LJM partnerships become dumping ground for concealing losses resulting from Enron's failed business ventures. LJM transactions wind up boosting Enron's reported financial results by more than $1 billion and enrich Fastow and coinvestors.

First hedging transaction between Enron and LJM occurs. Over the coming year, Enron enters into more than 20 distinct transactions with LJM partnerships.

Enron's Bolivia-to-Brazil natural gas pipeline is completed and begins operation. Its construction was one of the largest gas projects ever undertaken in South America.

Enron sells interest in Enron Oil & Gas but retains its China and India assets.

Fastow's LJM2 partnership is formed.

Enron completes its first bandwidth trade.

EES reports its first profitable quarter.

2000

February *Fortune* names Enron "The Most Innovative Company in America" for the fifth consecutive year. Enron launches EnronCredit.com, the first real-time credit department for corporations.

April Enron creates first controversial Raptor partnership—one of four that would hide $1 billion in losses.

May Ben Glisan becomes Enron's treasurer with success of Rhythms hedge seemingly fresh in management's collective mind.

August Rebecca Mark resigns from Enron. Mark's poor results at Azurix and other deals have given Skilling, her rival, an opportunity to push her

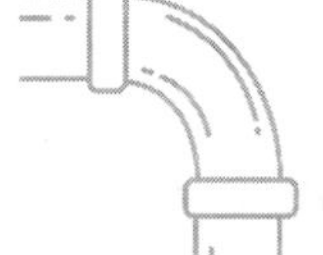

out. Mark had once been part of Lay's elite Office of the Chairman before being outmaneuvered by Skilling.

Through the year, Enron quietly attempts selling many of its international assets to raise cash and step up efforts in new markets such as broadband.

Enron stock hits all-time high of $90 a share in August. Analysts bite on Enron's potential promise in broadband. Stock selling by top executives begins in earnest.

Enron's revenue tops $100 billion for first time, making it the seventh largest company in the Fortune 500.

Enron launches the New Power Company to provide retail electricity to small business and residential customers. Skilling and Pai are major stakeholders.

Raptor special purpose entities (SPEs) created, expanding on the idea of the Rhythms transaction done by Enron and LJM in June 1999. LJM2 provides the outside equity designed to avoid consolidation of the Raptor SPEs into the Enron balance sheet. Enron used this strategy to avoid recognizing losses at the time.

November Enron had entered into derivative transactions with Raptors I, II, and III of over $1.5 billion notional. While Enron calculated its net gain on these deals to be slightly over $500 million, Enron could recognize these gains only if the Raptors could make good on their debt to Enron.

Enron's reported pretax earnings for last two quarters of 2000 total $650 million. "Earnings" from questionable Raptor deals account for more than 80 percent of this total. But two Raptor partnerships lack sufficient credit capacity to pay Enron on its "hedges," which Watkins later discovers.

2001

February Skilling assumes the post of CEO. Lay remains chairman, but some expect retirement or a political appointment.

March Raptor deals restructured so Enron can record only $36.6 million credit reserve loss, not $504 million.

Major broadband deal between Enron and Blockbuster collapses in March. But, using aggressive accounting practices, Enron records $111 million profit from the deal even though it never closed.

Credit capacity of Raptor transactions continues to decline, meaning they do not truly hedge Enron against risk. Income reported as a result of Raptor deals is not accurately reported, as a result.

Enron does not take charge against earnings of $500 million to reflect Raptor shortfalls, though it probably should have.

Fortune prints major article about Enron with headline "Is Enron Overpriced?" Stock slide continues.

According to then Enron treasurer Jeffrey McMahon in Congressional testimony, he approaches CEO Skilling with concerns about Enron's dealings with Raptor/LJM partnerships and non-arm's-length dealing by Fastow. Skilling relocates McMahon to executive position within Enron Industrial Markets. (Skilling said his recollection of the March 16 meeting was different when testifying at Congressional hearings in February 2002.)

April Skilling makes famous "asshole" comment during Wall Street analyst conference call.

Enron reports it is owed $570 million by bankrupt Californian power utility Pacific Gas & Electric.

August 14 CEO Skilling resigns from Enron after six months as CEO "for personal reasons."

August 15 Ken Lay assumes CEO position again, with stock trading at around $42 per share. (Stock later slips below $40 amid growing fears over the quality of Enron's earnings.)

Sherron Watkins, an accountant in Enron's finance division, sends anonymous memo to Ken Lay, warning of potential accounting scandals at Enron. Lay appoints law firm Vinson & Elkins to conduct "preliminary" investigation. Watkins notifies colleague of same concerns on August 20.

September Arthur Andersen requires Enron to reverse its aggressive accounting treatment, leading to $1.2 billion reduction of Enron's equity.

October 16 Securities and Exchange Commission (SEC) starts to investigate Enron's off-balance-sheet partnerships after Enron reports writing off over $1 billion on investments, and millions as a result of board-approved Fastow partnerships.

Lay calls U.S. Treasury Department to discuss company's situation.

October 17 Enron changes 401(k) pension plan administrator. This prevents participants from selling Enron stock for 30 days, which proves disastrous for Enron employees.

October 24 Fastow takes "leave of absence" in wake of controversy surrounding Enron's off-balance-sheet partnerships.

October 25 Enron reports drawing on $1 billion credit line to reassure investors that it won't face liquidity crisis. Investors react by selling.

October 28 Enron sets up special investigation committee to look into third-party transactions. The study, known as the Powers Report, is released in February 2002. The report documents some shortcomings by Enron's board of directors and management.

October 31 SEC investigation intensifies as Enron's stock price slumps to $11, its lowest point in nine years.

The media charges that the Chewco transaction was highly suspect, prompting the Enron board to seek briefing by management.

November 8 Chewco problems force Enron to restate earnings from 1997 through 2002, revealing $1.2 billion equity write-down. Company's debt burden increases dramatically as a result of its off-balance-sheet partnership disclosures.

November 9 Sensing it's in trouble, Enron strikes merger deal with Dynegy, its largest energy-industry rival.

Credit downgrade requires Enron to pay off more than $690 million debt immediately rather than in 2003, as it had planned. Dynegy gets cold feet and backs out of deal, as further problems at Enron become known.

November 28 Enron stock trades at less than $1 a share.

December 2 Enron files for Chapter 11 bankruptcy protection. Unlike Chapter 7, which requires liquidation, Chapter 11 gives corporations a period of time to reorganize and emerge from bankruptcy. Enron lays off 4,000 employees. Enron's stock is worthless. Current and former employees complain publicly about personal financial problems due to their 401(k) retirement investments being in now worthless Enron stock.

2002

January 10 Justice Department confirms it is conducting its own criminal investigation into Enron.

January 11 Enron's energy trading business is sold to UBS Warburg for one-third equity participation in its profits.

January 23 Lay resigns.

January 25 Former Enron Vice Chairman Cliff Baxter is found dead as government investigation intensifies.

February 7 Skilling testifies before Congress.

February 12 Lay appears before Congress and pleads the Fifth Amendment, just as Andersen's Duncan and Enron's Fastow, Kopper, and Glisan have done before.

February 14 Watkins testifies before Congress about her memo to Ken Lay.

April 8 Andersen layoffs reach 7,000 as firm's reputation suffers and major clients depart.

April 19 Jeffrey McMahon announces he will resign June 1 as president and CEO of Enron. McMahon was named to the posts after Enron declared bankruptcy in December. McMahon's departure comes after Enron creditors questioned his role in financing deals that inflated profits and hid losses before bankruptcy.

Judge overseeing Enron's bankruptcy case allows Justice Department to remove company executives as trustees of employees' retirement plan and hire an independent money manager.

The Enron Files

The publicly available documents surrounding Enron are fascinating to read for the first time (or to reread) once you have been told the larger story of Enron's fall into bankruptcy. From Sherron Watkins' first "anonymous" memo to Ken Lay to another memo that explores some of Enron's trading strategies in California, all of these documents offer deeper insight into the Enron story and the key characters who remain part of the still-unfolding news drama.

Admittedly, reproducing an old e-mail or someone's handwritten notes raises the question of whether it is better to typeset these materials to make them easier to read or to provide them to you in their original, unaltered form. In this instance, we have chosen authenticity. Some of these documents will satisfy your curiosity; others may have the power to shape your opinion about what actually happened and who was responsible. Most of these records and the events surrounding them have been discussed. To provide you with some further context we've included brief descriptions, with relevant background, on them:

File 1. Sherron Watkins' "anonymous" memo to Ken Lay. This document reportedly ended up in Ken Lay's hands on August 15, 2001, the day after Jeff Skilling resigned and Wall Street questioned Skilling's motives. Soon after the document was rumored to be leaked to Congress around January 12, 2002, Enron became not only the largest bankruptcy in U.S. history but a full-blown corporate scandal in the eyes of the public. The first wave of Congressional hearings were called.

File 2. Sherron Watkins' memo to the Enron public relations department on how Ken Lay should handle the financial mess. Dated October 30, 2001, this memo documents the PR spin that Watkins recommends that Lay use in his attempts to restore public confidence in Enron. The contents of the e-mail openly raise the question of whether Watkins was a "whistle-blower" in the purest sense.

File 3. LJM approval sheet with Jeff Skilling's signature missing. Enron reportedly was a company of rigorous risk management controls, and Skilling described himself as a "controls freak," not a "control freak," before Congress. A hotly debated question is just how much he knew about the most controversial LJM partnership transactions, and which deals should have required his approval. He was grilled about this during Congressional hearings. In his defense, Skilling argued that such deals were approved by Enron's outside accountant, Arthur Andersen, and repeated over and over the now famous line, "I am not an accountant."

File 4. A printout of Jeff McMahon's calendar showing the 11:30 A.M. meeting with Jeff Skilling on March 16, 2001. McMahon's calendar documents a meeting with Jeff Skilling, in which McMahon testified before Congress about "LJM situation in which AF [Andrew Fastow] wears two hats and upside comp[ensation] . . . creates a conflict I am right in the middle of." In talking point number three McMahon notes, "Will not compromise my integrity." Shortly after this meeting, McMahon was relocated within Enron's executive ranks.

File 5. Jeff McMahon's handwritten notes for his meeting with Jeff Skilling. Despite McMahon's discussion points in Enron File 4, Skilling testified before Congress that his recollection of this meeting differed from McMahon's. He remembered the meeting being largely about McMahon's "bonus."

File 6. Ken Lay's memo to Enron after Jeff Skilling's resignation. On the day that Skilling resigned, Lay tells Enron employees "that I have never felt better about the prospects for the company." This August 14 e-mail argues that Enron has never been stronger and clearly stands in stark contrast to the warnings made in Watkins' "anonymous" memo in Enron File 1.

File 7. Nancy Temple's memo about document retention forwarded to David Duncan in Andersen's Houston office. Whether Arthur Andersen simply followed its document retention policy or shredded valuable Enron-related documents illegally is being argued in the courts. This internal e-mail was forwarded to David Duncan, the Andersen partner in charge on the Enron account, to remind him of Andersen's retention policy.

File 8. Questions for Ken Lay from Representative Henry Waxman. Just one month after Enron's bankruptcy on December 4, 2001, Rep. Waxman asks some pointed questions of the former Enron chairman.

File 9. J. Clifford Baxter's purported suicide note.

File 10. Note from Kenneth Lay's lawyer, Earl J. Silbert, to Senator Ernest "Fritz" Hollings rescinding Lay's agreement to testify before Hollings' committee. Lay declines to testify before Congress on the grounds that he has already been prejudged.

File 11. Memo about Enron's trading strategies in California wholesale power markets. Documents some of the controversial trading strategies that Enron used in California.

File 1 Sherron Watkins' "anonymous" memo to Ken Lay.

Dear Mr. Lay,

Has Enron become a risky place to work? For those of us who didn't get rich over the last few years, can we afford to stay?

Skilling's abrupt departure will raise suspicions of accounting improprieties and valuation issues. Enron has been very aggressive in its accounting – most notably the Raptor transactions and the Condor vehicle. We do have valuation issues with our international assets and possibly some of our EES MTM positions.

The spotlight will be on us, the market just can't accept that Skilling is leaving his dream job. I think that the valuation issues can be fixed and reported with other goodwill write-downs to occur in 2002. How do we fix the Raptor and Condor deals? They unwind in 2002 and 2003, we will have to pony up Enron stock and that won't go unnoticed.

To the layman on the street, it will look like we recognized funds flow of $800 mm from merchant asset sales in 1999 by selling to a vehicle (Condor) that we capitalized with a promise of Enron stock in later years. Is that really funds flow or is it cash from equity issuance?

We have recognized over $550 million of fair value gains on stocks via our swaps with Raptor, much of that stock has declined significantly – Avici by 98%, from $178 mm to $5 mm, The New Power Co by 70%, from $20/share to $6/share. The value in the swaps won't be there for Raptor, so once again Enron will issue stock to offset these losses. Raptor is an LJM entity. It sure looks to the layman on the street that we are hiding losses in a related company and will compensate that company with Enron stock in the future.

I am incredibly nervous that we will implode in a wave of accounting scandals. My 8 years of Enron work history will be worth nothing on my resume, the business world will consider the past successes as nothing but an elaborate accounting hoax. Skilling is resigning now for 'personal reasons' but I think he wasn't having fun, looked down the road and knew this stuff was unfixable and would rather abandon ship now than resign in shame in 2 years.

Is there a way our accounting guru's can unwind these deals now? I have thought and thought about how to do this, but I keep bumping into one big problem – we booked the Condor and Raptor deals in 1999 and 2000, we enjoyed a wonderfully high stock price, many executives sold stock, we then try and reverse or fix the deals in 2001 and it's a bit like robbing the bank in one year and trying to pay back it back 2 years later. Nice try, but investors were hurt, they bought at $70 and $80/share looking for $120/share and now they're at $38 or worse. We are under too much scrutiny and there are probably one or two disgruntled 'redeployed' employees who know enough about the 'funny' accounting to get us in trouble.

What do we do? I know this question cannot be addressed in the all employee meeting, but can you give some assurances that you and Causey will sit down and take a good hard objective look at what is going to happen to Condor and Raptor in 2002 and 2003?

File 1 (Continued)

Summary of alleged issues:

Raptor

Entity was capitalized with LJM equity. That equity is at risk; however, the investment was completely offset by a cash fee paid to LJM. If the Raptor entities go bankrupt LJM is not affected, there is no commitment to contribute more equity.

The majority of the capitalization of the Raptor entities is some form of Enron N/P, restricted stock and stock rights.

Enron entered into several equity derivative transactions with the Raptor entities locking in our values for various equity investments we hold.

As disclosed, in 2000, we recognized $500 million of revenue from the equity derivatives offset by market value changes in the underlying securities.

This year, with the value of our stock declining, the underlying capitalization of the Raptor entities is declining and Credit is pushing for reserves against our MTM positions.

To avoid such a write-down or reserve in Q1 2001, we 'enhanced' the capital structure of the Raptor vehicles, committing more ENE shares.

My understanding of the Q3 problem is that we must 'enhance' the vehicles by $250 million.

I realize that we have had a lot of smart people looking at this and a lot of accountants including AA&Co. have blessed the accounting treatment. None of that will protect Enron if these transactions are ever disclosed in the bright light of day. (Please review the late 90's problems of Waste Management – where AA paid $130+ mm in litigation re: questionable accounting practices).

The overriding basic principle of accounting is that if you explain the 'accounting treatment' to a man on the street, would you influence his investing decisions? Would he sell or buy the stock based on a thorough understanding of the facts? If so, you best present it correctly and/or change the accounting.

My concern is that the footnotes don't adequately explain the transactions. If adequately explained, the investor would know that the "Entities" described in our related party footnote are thinly capitalized, the equity holders have no skin in the game, and all the value in the entities comes from the underlying value of the derivatives (unfortunately in this case, a big loss) AND Enron stock and N/P. Looking at the stock we swapped, I also don't believe any other company would have entered into the equity derivative transactions with us at the same prices or without substantial premiums from Enron. In other words, the $500 million in revenue in 2000 would have been much lower. How much lower?

File 1 (Continued)

Raptor looks to be a big bet, if the underlying stocks did well, then no one would be the wiser. If Enron stock did well, the stock issuance to these entities would decline and the transactions would be less noticeable. All has gone against us. The stocks, most notably Hanover, The New Power Co., and Avici are underwater to great or lesser degrees.

I firmly believe that executive management of the company must have a clear and precise knowledge of these transactions and they must have the transactions reviewed by objective experts in the fields of securities law and accounting. I believe Ken Lay deserves the right to judge for himself what he believes the probabilities of discovery to be and the estimated damages to the company from those discoveries and decide one of two courses of action:

1. The probability of discovery is low enough and the estimated damage too great; therefore we find a way to quietly and quickly reverse, unwind, write down these positions/transactions.
2. The probability of discovery is too great, the estimated damage to the company too great; therefore, we must quantify, develop damage containment plans and disclose.

I firmly believe that the probability of discovery significantly increased with Skilling's shocking departure. Too many people are looking for a smoking gun.

File 1 (Continued)

Summary of Raptor oddities:

1. The accounting treatment looks questionable.

   a. Enron booked a $500 mm gain from equity derivatives from a related party.
   b. That related party is thinly capitalized, with no party at risk except Enron.
   c. It appears Enron has supported an income statement gain by a contribution of its own shares.

   One basic question: The related party entity has lost $500 mm in its equity derivative transactions with Enron. Who bears that loss? I can't find an equity or debt holder that bears that loss. Find out who will lose this money. Who will pay for this loss at the related party entity?

   If it's Enron, from our shares, then I think we do not have a fact pattern that would look good to the SEC or investors.

2. The equity derivative transactions do not appear to be at arms length.

   a. Enron hedged New Power, Hanover, and Avici with the related party at what now appears to be the peak of the market. New Power and Avici have fallen away significantly since. The related party was unable to lay off this risk. This fact pattern is once again very negative for Enron.
   b. I don't think any other unrelated company would have entered into these transactions at these prices. What else is going on here? What was the compensation to the related party to induce it to enter into such transactions?

3. There is a veil of secrecy around LJM and Raptor. Employees question our accounting propriety consistently and constantly. This alone is cause for concern.

   a. Jeff McMahon was highly vexed over the inherent conflicts of LJM. He complained mightily to Jeff Skilling and laid out 5 steps he thought should be taken if he was to remain as Treasurer. 3 days later, Skilling offered him the CEO spot at Enron Industrial Markets and never addressed the 5 steps with him.
   b. Cliff Baxter complained mightily to Skilling and all who would listen about the inappropriateness of our transactions with LJM.
   c. I have heard one manager level employee from the principle investments group say "I know it would be devastating to all of us, but I wish we would get caught. We're such a crooked company." The principle investments group hedged a large number of their investments with Raptor. These people know and see a lot. Many similar comments are made when you ask about these deals. Employees quote our CFO as saying that he has a handshake deal with Skilling that LJM will never lose money.

File 1 (Continued)

4. Can the General Counsel of Enron audit the deal trail and the money trail between Enron and LJM/Raptor and its principals? Can he look at LJM? At Raptor? If the CFO says no, isn't that a problem?

File 1 (Continued)

Condor and Raptor work:

1. Postpone decision on filling office of the chair, if the current decision includes CFO and/or CAO.

2. Involve Jim Derrick and Rex Rogers to hire a law firm to investigate the Condor and Raptor transactions to give Enron attorney client privilege on the work product. (Can't use V&E due to conflict – they provided some true sale opinions on some of the deals).

3. Law firm to hire one of the big 6, but not Arthur Andersen or PricewaterhouseCoopers due to their conflicts of interest: AA&Co (Enron); PWC (LJM).

4. Investigate the transactions, our accounting treatment and our future commitments to these vehicles in the form of stock, N/P, etc..
For instance: In Q3 we have a $250 mm problem with Raptor 3 (NPW) if we don't 'enhance' the capital structure of Raptor 3 to commit more ENE shares. By the way: in Q1 we enhanced the Raptor 3 deal, committing more ENE shares to avoid a write down.

5. Develop clean up plan:

   a. Best case: Clean up quietly if possible.

   b. Worst case: Quantify, develop PR and IR campaigns, customer assurance plans (don't want to go the way of Salomon's trading shop), legal actions, severance actions, disclosure.

6. Personnel to quiz confidentially to determine if I'm all wet:
   a. Jeff McMahon
   b. Mark Koenig
   c. Rick Buy
   d. Greg Whalley

File 1 (Continued)

To put the accounting treatment in perspective I offer the following:

1. We've contributed contingent Enron equity to the Raptor entities. Since it's contingent, we have the consideration given and received at zero. We do, as Causey points out, include the shares in our fully diluted computations of shares outstanding if the current economics of the deal imply that Enron will have to issue the shares in the future. This impacts 2002 – 2004 EPS projections only.

2. We lost value in several equity investments in 2000. $500 million of lost value. These were fair value investments, we wrote them down. However, we also booked gains from our price risk management transactions with Raptor, recording a corresponding PRM account receivable from the Raptor entities. That's a $500 million related party transaction – it's 20% of 2000 IBIT, 51% of NI pre tax, 33% of NI after tax.

3. Credit reviews the underlying capitalization of Raptor, reviews the contingent shares and determines whether the Raptor entities will have enough capital to pay Enron its $500 million when the equity derivatives expire.

4. The Raptor entities are technically bankrupt; the value of the contingent Enron shares equals or is just below the PRM account payable that Raptor owes Enron. Raptor's inception to date income statement is a $500 million loss.

5. Where are the equity and debt investors that lost out? LJM is whole on a cash on cash basis. Where did the $500 million in value come from? It came from Enron shares. Why haven't we booked the transaction as $500 million in a promise of shares to the Raptor entity and $500 million of value in our "Economic Interests" in these entities? Then we would have a write down of our value in the Raptor entities. We have not booked the latter, because we do not have to yet. Technically, we can wait and face the music in 2002 – 2004.

6. The related party footnote tries to explain these transactions. Don't you think that several interested companies, be they stock analysts, journalists, hedge fund managers, etc., are busy trying to discover the reason Skilling left? Don't you think their smartest people are pouring over that footnote disclosure right now? I can just hear the discussions – "It looks like they booked a $500 million gain from this related party company and I think, from all the undecipherable ½ page on Enron's contingent contributions to this related party entity, I think the related party entity is capitalized with Enron stock." ..... "No, no, no, you must have it all wrong, it can't be that, that's just too bad, too fraudulent, surely AA&Co wouldn't let them get away with that?" ..... "Go back to the drawing board, it's got to be something else. But find it!" ...... "Hey, just in case you might be right, try and find some insiders or 'redeployed' former employees to validate your theory."

File 2 Sherron Watkins' memo to the Enron public relations department on how Ken Lay should handle the financial mess.

21

Watkins, Sherron

From: Watkins, Sherron
Sent: Tuesday, October 30, 2001 4:45 PM
To: Tilney, Elizabeth
Cc: Olson, Cindy
Subject: PR for Enron

Beth,

Attached is the handout I gave Ken Lay today in our very brief meeting; I think I left you a voice mail on this.

Ken thinks it would be a good idea for me to work for you in our PR and IR efforts re: our current crisis. Beth I think you know my involvement from Cindy, and that I haven't really had a real job since my first meeting with Ken re: these matters in late August. I can jump on this asap.

The viewpoint is that I can effectively play devil's advocate on the accounting issues and be sure we anticipate the tough questions and have answers. My personal opinion is that it's very hard to know who in the organization is giving us good answers and who's covering their prior work.

The attached outlines my viewpoint on the fact that I think we need to come clean and restate; Ken and I did not get much chance to discuss this; I'm tentatively on his schedule Wed afternoon. I'd sure like to meet with you on this. I have one meeting on Wed that I can change. Please call. Thanks.

Disclosure steps to rebuild in...

Sherron S. Watkins
Vice President, Enron Corp.
713-345-8799 office
713-416-0620 cell

Private placement Opp

1. S/T Capital/Credit
2. L/T " / " Equity
3. SEC
4. Capital Mkts — Don't put SEC 3rd!

SW(HSE&EC)0023

1

File 2 (Continued)

Disclosure steps to rebuild investor confidence:

1. Lay to be open about his involvement or more importly, his lack thereof:

   a. As CEO, he relied on his COO, Skilling, as well as CFO, Fastow and CAO, Causey, to manage the details. Of note: CFO and CAO are Skilling's picks from his rise to the COO spot in late 1996.

   [It's fairly normal for a CEO to leave the accounting details and finance details to the COO, CFO and CAO]

   b. Lay to admit that he trusted the wrong people.

2. Lay to admit that as soon as Skilling resigned employees reported to him their opinions as to the inappropriate LJM transactions.

   a. Lay appropriately took the matter seriously and he began an investigation; however:

   b. Mistake #2: He relied on V&E and Arthur Andersen to opine on their own work. They advised him to unwind Raptor, but that the accounting was appropriate when recorded in 2000.

   Joe Dilg's Oct 16th comment to me when I said that Lay should probably come clean and admit problems and restate 2000, in order to preserve his legacy and possibly the company's was the following:

   "Are you suggesting that Ken Lay should ignore the advise of his counsel and auditors concerning this matter?"

3. Lay to state that once the 3rd Quarter write downs and reversals were disclosed and investors raised concerns and it became apparent that Enron could not easily resolve the issues by making more detail disolosures, he realized that the advise from V&E and AA&Co was wrong, it was motivated by self preservation.

   a. First, the LJM Raptor transactions were highly irregular and Enron is restating 2000 financials.
   b. Second, he's firing Arthur Andersen & Co and V&E
   c. Third, he's committed to staying at Enron and returning the company to its former glory.

   NOTE: After restatement, the good news is that our core trading business is solid with strong numbers to report; the bad news: EBS was losing big

SW(HSE&EC)0024

File 2 (Continued)

money in 2000, the big losses didn't start in 2001, and EES did not start making a profit in 2000.

4. Lay to meet with top SEC officials. This is a problem we must all address and fix for corporate America as a whole. Ken Lay and his board were duped by a COO who wanted the targets met no matter what the consequences, a CFO motivated by personal greed and 2 of the most respected firms, AA&Co and V&E, who had both grown too wealthy off Enron's yearly business and no longer performed their roles as Ken Lay, the Board and just about anybody on the street would expect as a minimum standard for CPA's and attorneys.

    a. This is devastating to many – investors, the energy trading sector, the banking sector, the Houston economy – Enron could work with the SEC to develop a plan to address this calmly.
    b. Ken Lay and Enron need to support one of the SEC's long term objectives of requiring that the Big 5 accounting firms rotate off their large clients on a regular basis as short as 3 years.

<u>My conclusions if Ken Lay takes these steps:</u>

1. The bad news: This is horrific. Plaintiff attorneys will be celebrating. The trouble facing the company will be obvious to all.
2. The good news: the wild speculations will slow down, if not cease. Nobody wants Ken Lay's head. He's very well respected in business and the community. The culprits are Skilling, Fastow, Glisan and Causey as well as Arthur Andersen and V&E. The energy trading sector is scared to death that Enron won't make it – there will not be a cry for Enron's collective head.

<u>Likely Enron outcome:</u>
The stock price will drop further
Hard to take over – it's people and trading business (ie, not contractual, not asset based)
Does Enron need to find a Warren Buffet type equity investor?
Can we build a ring around the trading business? How long will that take?
Will a restatement announcement hurt liquidity any more than our current situation?

<u>My conclusions if we don't come clean and restate:</u>

All these bad things will happen to us anyway, it's just that Ken Lay will be more implicated in this than is deserved and he won't get the chance to restore the company to its former stature.

~~Public~~ Investor opinion
Tried in the Court
+ we won't succeed

SW(HSE&EC)0025

File 3 LJM approval sheet with Jeff Skilling's signature missing.

LJM2 APPROVAL SHEET

This Approval Sheet should be used to approve Enron's participation in any transactions involving LJM Cayman, L.P. ("LJM1") or LJM2 Co-Investment, L.P. ("LJM2"). LJM1 and LJM2 will collectively be referred to as "LJM". This Approval Sheet is in addition to (not in lieu of) any other Enron approvals that may be required.

GENERAL

Deal name: Raptor

Date Approval Sheet completed: April 18, 2000

Enron person completing this form: Trushar Patel

Expected closing date: May 4, 2000

Business Unit: Enron Corp.

Business Unit Originator: Ben Glisan

This transaction relates to ☐LJM1 and/or ☑LJM2.

This transaction is ☐ a sale by Enron ☐a purchase by Enron ☐a co-sale with Enron ☐a co-purchase with Enron and/or ☑other:__creation of hedging structure_________.

Person(s) negotiating for Enron: Ben Glisan

Person(s) negotiating for LJM: Michael Kopper

Legal counsel for Enron: Vinson & Elkins

Legal counsel for LJM: Kirkland & Ellis

DEAL DESCRIPTION

Talon I LLC ("Talon") is a special purpose entity organized for the purpose of entering into certain derivative transactions. LJM2, through its 100% voting control of Talon, has the unilateral ability to make the investment decisions for Talon and is not contractually obligated to execute any derivative transactions with Enron. LJM2 will execute derivative transactions with Harrier I LLC ("Harrier"), a wholly-owned subsidiary of Enron, to the extent those investment decisions are aligned with LJM2's investment objectives. Enron, through Harrier, will offer LJM2 the opportunity to execute derivative instruments relating to both public and private energy and telecommunication investments made by Enron.

ECONOMICS

Talon's distributions to equity holders will be limited by earnings at Talon. To the extent there are earnings and sufficient cash to distribute, distributions will be made according to the following waterfall:

- First, $41 million to LJM2
- Second, distributions as necessary until LJM2 receives a 30% IRR over the term of the structure (unless the IRR was achieved through the $41 million distribution above)
- Third, 100% to the special limited partnership interest, Harrier I LLC, a wholly-owned subsidiary of Enron

DASH

See attached.

VEL 00129

\\ahou-svr1\cloehr$\Raptor_LJMApproval.doc

File 3 (Continued)

LJM APPROVAL SHEET
Page 2

ISSUES CHECKLIST

1. Sale Options
   a. If this transaction is a sale of an asset by Enron, which of the following options were considered and rejected:
   ☐Condor ☐JEDI II ☐Third Party ☐Direct Sale. Please explain: Not a sale of an asset by Enron
   b. Will this transaction be the most beneficial alternative to Enron? ☑Yes ☐No. If no, please explain:__________
   c. Were any other bids/offers received in connection with this transaction? ☐Yes ☑No. Please explain: Private structured finance transaction
2. Prior Obligations
   a. Does this transaction involve a Qualified Investment (as defined in the JEDI II partnership agreement)? ☐Yes ☑No. If yes, please explain how this issue was resolved: __________.
   b. Was this transaction required to be offered to any other Enron affiliate or other party pursuant to a contractual or other obligation? ☐Yes ☑No. If yes, please explain: __________.
3. Terms of Transaction
   a. What are the benefits (financial and otherwise) to Enron in this transaction? ☐Cash flow ☐Earnings
   ☑Other: Ability to hedge mark-to-market exposure on investments in publicly and privately held companies
   b. Was this transaction done strictly on an arm's-length basis? ☑Yes ☐No. If no, please explain:__________.
   c. Was Enron advised by any third party that this transaction was not fair, from a financial perspective, to Enron? ☐Yes ☑No. If yes, please explain:__________.
   d. Are all LJM expenses and out-of-pocket costs (including legal fees) being paid by LJM? ☐Yes ☑No. If no, is this market standard or has the economic impact of paying any expenses and out-of-pocket costs been considered when responding to items 1.b. and 3.b. above? ☑Yes ☐No.
4. Compliance
   a. Will this transaction require disclosure as a Certain Transaction in Enron's proxy statement? ☑Yes ☐No.
   b. Will this transaction result in any compensation (as defined by the proxy rules) being paid to any Enron employee? ☐Yes ☑No.
   c. Have all Enron employees' involvement in this transaction on behalf of LJM been waived by Enron's Office of the Chairman in accordance with Enron's Conduct of Business Affairs Policy? ☑Yes ☐No. If no, please explain: __________.
   d. Was this transaction reviewed and approved by Enron's Chief Accounting Officer? ☑Yes ☐No.
   e. Was this transaction reviewed and approved by Enron's Chief Risk Officer? ☑Yes ☐No.
   f. Has the Audit Committee of the Enron Corp. Board of Directors reviewed all Enron/LJM transactions within the past twelve months? ☐Yes ☑No. (The Audit Committee has not held a meeting since LJM2's formation.) Have all recommendations of the Audit Committee relating to Enron/LJM transactions been taken into account in this transaction? ☐Yes ☐No.

VEL 00130

H:\Raptor_LJMApproval.doc

File 3 (Continued)

LJM APPROVAL SHEET
Page 3

APPROVALS	Name	Signature	Date
Business Unit	Ben Glisan	[signature]	6-12-00
Business Unit Legal			
Enron Corp. Legal	Rex Rogers	[signature]	5-24-00
Global Finance Legal	Scott Sefton	Scott Sefton	5-22-00
RAC	Rick Buy DBG	[signature]	5-22-00
Accounting	Rick Causey	[signature]	5-22-00
Executive	Jeff Skilling		

VEL 00131

H:\Raptor_LJMApproval.doc

File 4 **A printout of Jeff McMahon's calendar showing the 11:30 A.M. meeting with Jeff Skilling on March 16, 2001.**

PAGE 3/

March 2000 - April 2000

Monday	Tuesday	Wednesday	Thursday	Friday
March 6 10:00am Tim DeSpain, Bill 12:00pm Arena Finance 2:00pm Ken Rice, Kevin 3:00pm Thomas Sloop - 3:45pm Mike Jakubik - 4:00pm Harry Aurora & Tim 6:30pm Avanti to pick you	7 8:00am Utendahl Capital Mtg w/ Dana Reed, John 11:00am Barry Schnapper - Contracts 11:30am Flight to New York 7:30pm Dinner in NY - John	8 8:00am Moody's mtg - Stephen Moore, 9:00am Sue Dentist 10:30am Tom Blair - Bear 1:00pm Bank of New York , 3:00pm Leave New York for 4:50pm CO51 from	9 8:30am Andy Meinell 9:00am McKinsey - Suzanne 10:00am DG Bank mtg- Mark 11:30am Lunch w/Mike 2:00pm XBC - Mike Sawicki, 3:00pm Joe Kishkill - Update	10 8:00am MOVE DAY TO 50TH............... 11:00am Lunch, Grill Room at the Houston Country Club for 12:15 p.m.Tea time is for 1
13 9:40am Urgent Call Mike Jakubik 713 899 10:00am Bill & Shirley - your 12:00pm Lunch w/ Bill - 2:00pm Mark Schroeder 3:00pm Mary Perkins - 4:00pm Harry Arora.	14 10:30am Jedi & Orca Mtg - Andy & Shirley Hu 11:00am Greg Whalley - 12:00pm 12:30 table booked 2:00pm Credit Conference 3:00pm Charlene Jackson & 4:00pm JP Morgan- John	8:30am Rick Walker Gleysteen. 9:30am Mees Pierso Michael Da 1:00pm Terry Darby 1:30pm Andy 3:00pm Dave Dunca	16 8:30am Ray Bowen - Ray's 10:30am Conf Call w/John 11:30am Jeff Skilling, his office 1:00pm Hal Burtram - Project 1:30pm Jim Hunt SBC 2:00pm Jim Reilly - Update. 3:00pm Conf Call Roger	17 Scotia Bank - Barry Barry Schnapper, Turbine Sue & Amy (lunch Lunch will be Tim DeSpain, Bill Doug McDowell &
20 10:00am Jim McGinniss - Morgan Stanley (212 1:00pm John Sherriff - 2:30pm Joe Cunningham - Dain Raushel Wes 3:45pm Joe Sutton Re: 4:30pm Paul Cambridge	21 9:00am Jay Hellums - Update 10:00am Conf Call re: Teesside/EEP6 loan 10:30am Louie Fischer, Mike 11:30am Lunch w/Leo Paige & 1:00pm Greg Hall Re: 4:00pm Rick Causey - Couple	8:30am Ben Glisan 9:00am Jeff Thibault - Personal 10:30am Mark Koenig & Mark Muller re: Resco IPO. 1:30pm Dentist Appointment - Dr Turner (713 771	10:00am Kevin Howard and 11:30am Lunch w/ Larry 1:00pm Keith Marlow EECC 3:00pm Mike McConnell my	24 Harry Arora - Update. Mike McConnell & David Pope. 11:30am Lunch - Bob Schorr meet in lobby. 11:30am Sue & Amy - Bridget taking us for welcom
27 10:00am Larry Derrett - Deal structure 12:00pm Lunch in my off with Tim DeSpain Sue to 3:00pm Greg Cardenas - (C 503-539 7633) Opp 7:00pm Dinner with Mark	28 6:00am Avanti to pick up at 6:45am. All day trip to Chicago with Causey Flight info CO1714 7:45am wi	29 10:00am Tier Two Outing -Barton Creek	30 10:00am Tier Two Outing -Barton Creek 10:00am Flight from Austin to Houston CO1955 departs at 12.29pm arrives Houston 1:26pm Avanti to tak	31 7:00am Sue will be out today. 7:30am Meeting with Andy 9:30am Conf Call - Kimberly 11:00am Interview for 11:30am Meeting with Jeff 12:00pm Lunch - Mary Joyce 7:05pm Astros v Yankees
3 12:00pm Lunch w/ Tim DeSpain 2:00pm Interview with Bill Nordlund, (Dan Castagnola's group) 4:00pm Cheryl Lipshutz Re: Instutional Investor	4 9:00am Thomas Sloop 10:00am Scott Gaiselman, 11:30am Cheryl Lipshutz 12:30pm Lunch W/ Eric Herbst 2:00pm Louie Fischer & Mike 3:00pm John Miller JP Morgan 4:00pm Ray Bowen - Update	5 11:00am Mike Jakubik 11:30am Bill Brown 12:00pm Jeff's Staff mtg - Bill, 1:30pm Barry Schnapper 2:15pm Brian Manonles he 3:00pm Paul Chivers - he will 3:30pm Andy - Capital	6 9:00am EGF - Operating Committee Mtg - 11:00am Conf Call - Jill Sakol and Terran Miller - 1:00pm Enron Net Works - Staff Mtg EB332(3:30pm 4pm Haircut - Cindy	7 8:00am Sue will be out today 9:00am Marlos 9:30am Bill Brown 10:00am Barry Schnapper 11:00am Floor Move Meeting E83320 Liz, Lori Bel 1:30pm 2 - 3pm - Parent/

McMahon, Jeffrey 1 2/6/2002

JM-HEC-00001

TOTAL P.02

File 5 Jeff McMahon's handwritten notes for his meeting with Jeff Skilling.

Discussion Points

1/ Untenable Situation

- LJM situation where AF wears 2 hats and upside comp is so great creates a conflict ~~that puts me in~~ I am right in the middle of.
- I find myself negotiating with Andy on Enron matters and am pressured to do a deal that I do not believe is in the best interests of the shareholders [Did not ask to be put in this position]

2/ Request/Options

(A) Where my integrity forces me to continue to negotiate the way I believe is correct - ~~to~~ [However AF is my boss].
- In order to continue to do this, I MUST KNOW I have support from you and there won't be any ramifications [believe it already has affected my comp]

OR

(B) Need to be move out of situation and go do something else in company. Will not compromise my integrity

***File 5* (Continued)**

Conflict Matters

1/ Terms and Pricing
- Follow thru on deals – who audit?

2/ Bank Impressions as to Debts owed

3/ Other Personnel Matters –
- ENE reporting to LJM
=> Same floor
- Staff Meeting Attendance
- Bonuses do get affected – MK, JM

4/ General Conflict Matter Resolution –
*Want to be able to speak freely and not do it behind the gloves via Joe S of Jeff S *

File 6 Ken Lay's memo to Enron after Jeff Skilling's resignation.

From: PGE News
To: ALL PGE EMPLOYEES
Date: 8/14/01 2:54PM
Subject: Jeff Skilling resigns as CEO of Enron

PGE News .... August 14, 2001

Jeff Skilling resigns as CEO of Enron

Enron today announced that President and CEO Jeff Skilling has resigned, effective immediately, and that the Enron Board of Directors has asked Ken Lay to resume his role as Chairman and CEO.

"Stan Horton called this afternoon to inform me of Jeff's decision to step down for personal reasons," says PGE CEO and President Peggy Fowler. Horton, CEO of Enron Transportation, is Fowler's executive connection to the Enron team. "He wanted to let me know that Mr. Skilling's departure will not in any way impact Enron's ongoing strategy for success and we should expect no near-term dramatic organizational changes."

"Clearly, Enron will continue to focus on increasing the company's stock value," Fowler added. "PGE can help in this effort by remaining committed to our Scorecard goals and operational excellence."

Below is the letter Ken Lay is sending to Enron employees this afternoon announcing the decision:

To: Enron Employees Worldwide
From: Ken Lay

It is with regret that I have to announce that Jeff Skilling is leaving Enron. Today, the Board of Directors accepted his resignation as President and CEO of Enron. Jeff is resigning for personal reasons and his decision is voluntary. I regret his decision, but I accept and understand it. I have worked closely with Jeff for more than 15 years, including 11 here at Enron, and have had few, if any, professional relationships that I value more. I am pleased to say that he has agreed to enter into a consulting arrangement with the company to advise me and the Board of Directors.

Now it's time to look forward.

With Jeff leaving, the Board has asked me to resume the responsibilities of President and CEO in addition to my role as Chairman of the Board. I have agreed. I want to assure you that I have never felt better about the prospects for the company. All of you know that our stock price has suffered substantially over the last few months. One of my top priorities will be to restore a significant amount of the stock value we have lost as soon as possible. Our performance has never been stronger; our business model has never been more robust; our growth has never been more certain; and most importantly, we have never had a better nor deeper pool of talent throughout the company. We have the finest organization in American business today. Together, we will make Enron the world's leading company.

CC: Kathy & George Wyatt; Kathy Wyatt

File 7 **Nancy Temple's memo about document retention forwarded to David Duncan in Andersen's Houston office.**

01/14/2002 15:56 FAX 212 450 6032 DPW 28-29

To: David B. Duncan@ANDERSEN WO
CC:
BCC:
Date: 10/12/2001 08:56 AM
From: Michael C. Odom
Subject: Document retention policy
Attachments:

More help.

----------------- Forwarded by Michael C. Odom on 10/12/2001 10:55 AM -----------------

To: Michael C. Odom@ANDERSEN WO
cc:
Date: 10/12/2001 10:53 AM
From: Nancy A Temple, Chicago 33 W. Monroe, 50 / 11234
Subject: Document retention policy

Mike-
It might be useful to consider reminding the engagement team of our documentation and retention policy. It will be helpful to make sure that we have complied with the policy. Let me know if you have any questions.

Nancy

http://www.intranet.andersen.com/onefirm.nsf/content/ResourcesFirmwidePoliciesPolicy-ClientInformationOrganization!OpenDocument

File 8 Questions for Ken Lay from Representative Henry Waxman.

ONE HUNDRED SEVENTH CONGRESS

Congress of the United States

House of Representatives

COMMITTEE ON GOVERNMENT REFORM

2157 RAYBURN HOUSE OFFICE BUILDING

WASHINGTON, DC 20515–6143

MAJORITY (202) 225–5074
FACSIMILE (202) 225–3974
MINORITY (202) 225–5051
TTY (202) 225–6852

www.house.gov/reform

January 12, 2002

Mr. Kenneth L. Lay
Chairman
Enron Corporation
1400 Smith St.
Houston, TX 77002

Dear Mr. Lay:

Since December 4, 2001, my staff has been investigating the collapse of Enron Corporation. An important component of this investigation is reaching out to current and former employees who might have relevant information. I have done this through the establishment of an Internet tip line, as well as through other means.

As a result of this investigation, I have obtained some e-mails that you purportedly sent out to Enron employees about Enron's financial condition and stock price in August 2001. Copies of these e-mails are enclosed. If it is true that you sent these e-mails, then it appears that you misled your employees into believing that Enron was prospering and that its stock price would rise:

- In an e-mail apparently sent to all employees on August 14, 2001, the day that Jeffrey Skilling resigned as CEO, you stated: "**I want to assure you that I have never felt better about the prospects for the company.** All of you know that our stock price has suffered substantially over the last few months. One of my top priorities will be to restore a significant amount of the stock value we have lost as soon as possible." You concluded: "**Our performance has never been stronger; our business model has never been more robust; our growth has never been more certain**.... **We have the finest organization in American business today.**"[1]

- In an e-mail on August 27, 2001, to employees who received a grant of stock options, you apparently said that "one of my highest priorities is to restore investor confidence in

[1]E-mail from Ken Lay to Enron Employees Worldwide (Aug. 14, 2001) (emphasis added).

File 8 (Continued)

Mr. Kenneth L. Lay
January 12, 2002
Page 2

Enron. **<u>This should result in a significantly higher stock price.</u>**"[2]

By the time of the second e-mail, when the stock price was $37, you had already sold $40 million of Enron stock during 2001 and over $100 million since October 1998.[3] The price of Enron stock eventually fell to a low of 26 cents a share on November 30, 2001.

If these e-mails are genuine, your pronouncements about Enron's financial condition and stock price stand in stark contrast to what is now known about Enron's precarious situation. They also stand in stark contrast to the statements you made to Secretary of the Treasury Paul H. O'Neill nine weeks later about Enron's dire financial condition. At a minimum, they create the appearance that you misled Enron employees about the value of their investments in Enron and the security of their jobs. If this were accurate, it would be a gross betrayal of your employees' trust, as well as possibly illegal conduct.

Clearly, the statements in these e-mail messages require further investigation. For this reason, I request that you:

(1) Please verify whether you sent the enclosed e-mails;

(2) If the e-mails are genuine, please explain whether you were aware when you sent them of Enron's financial vulnerabilities. If you were not aware of this, please explain whether this was because Jeffrey Skilling or other executives withheld that information from you;

(3) Please provide me with all records of internal Enron communications, including e-mails and videotapes, between August 14, 2001, and December 2, 2001, assessing the value of Enron's stock price or Enron's financial condition; and

(4) Please provide me with copies of all public statements by Enron executives between August 14, 2001, and December 2, 2001, regarding the value of Enron's stock price or Enron's financial condition.

I would also like to know about your decision to prevent participants in Enron's 401(k) plan from accessing their retirement accounts and selling their plummeting Enron stock. For this reason, I request that you provide all information relating to Enron's decision to establish the 401(k) lock-down. According to the *Wall Street Journal*, this lock-down began on October 17,

---

[2]E-mail from Ken Lay to Unnamed Employee (Aug. 27, 2001) (emphasis added).

[3]Class Action Complaint for Violations of the Federal Securities Laws, *Amalgamated Bank, et al., v. Kenneth Lay, et al.* (S.D. Tex. 2000).

File 8 (Continued)

Mr. Kenneth L. Lay
January 12, 2002
Page 3

2001, the day after Enron first revealed its financial difficulties.[4]

Finally, I would like you to explain why, after you allegedly sent the e-mails and subsequently spoke to Secretary O'Neill -- and as the company's stock continued to fall -- you still sought a $60-million severance package from Enron. As you will remember, when Enron employees objected to this, you proposed reducing your package to $40 million.[5] When Enron employees objected to that proposal, you finally decided in mid-November not to accept this compensation.[6]

I think it is essential that this information be provided so that there is a clear public accounting of this matter. We all owe that to the thousands of families that are facing financial ruin from the Enron bankruptcy. Accordingly, I would appreciate your providing this information by the close of business, January 18, 2002.

Sincerely,

Henry A. Waxman
Ranking Minority Member

Attachments

---

[4]*Fair Shares? Why Company Stock is a Burden for Many,* Wall Street Journal (Nov. 27, 2001).

[5]*Enron CEO Says No to $60.6 Million,* Washington Post (Nov. 14, 2001).

[6]*See id.; Lay To Forgo $60M Severance,* Gas Daily (Nov. 15, 2001); *Enron Chief Nixes $60 Million; Lay Decides Against Accepting Severance Package*, San Antonio Express-News (Nov. 14, 2001).

File 9 **J. Clifford Baxter's purported suicide note.**
Source: Houston Chronicle.

02000599

CAROL,

I AM SO SORRY FOR THIS. I FEEL I JUST CAN'T GO ON. I HAVE ALWAYS TRIED TO DO THE RIGHT THING BUT WHERE THERE WAS ONCE GREAT PRIDE NOW ITS GONE. I LOVE YOU AND THE CHILDREN SO MUCH. I JUST CAN'T BE ANY GOOD TO YOU OR MYSELF. THE PAIN IS OVERWHELMING.

PLEASE TRY TO FORGIVE ME.

CLIFF

J. Clifford Baxter

CAROL

File 10 Note from Kenneth Lay's lawyer, Earl J. Silbert, to Senator Ernest "Fritz" Hollings rescinding Lay's agreement to testify before Hollings' committee.

03 2002 9:28 AM FR NEW YORK TIMES 202 862 0427 TO 92244293 P.01
FEB 03 2002 17:18 FR PIPER MARBURY RUD 6H

1200 Nineteenth Street, N.W.
Washington, D.C. 20036-2412
www.piperrudnick.com

MAIN PHONE (202) 861-3900
FAX (202) 223-2085

Earl J. Silbert
earl.silbert@piperrudnick.com

DIRECT PHONE 202-861-6250
FAX 202-223-2085

February 3, 2002

Hon. Ernest Hollings, Chairman
Committee on Commerce, Science and Transportation
508 Dirksen Senate Office Building
Washington, DC 20510-6125

Dear Mr. Chairman:

About one month ago, Kenneth Lay accepted your invitation to appear before this committee and subcommittee to testify about the collapse of Enron. He was looking forward to a meaningful, reasoned question and answer session to provide his understanding of the events and to discuss with you a number of related policy, legal, and regulatory issues. This tragedy for the company, its current and prior employees, retirees, and shareholders has been devastating and heartbreaking to him.

Many allegations have been publicized in the news media accusing Mr. Lay and others of wrongful, even criminal conduct. He has not personally responded to them. Some have construed his silence as acquiescence. They are wrong. Mr. Lay firmly rejects any allegations that he engaged in wrongful or criminal conduct. He did and still does believe that the most appropriate place to explore these allegations and related policy issues was before the Congress.

Mr. Lay, with counsel, has been spending extensive time preparing both for written and oral testimony. As of this morning, Mr. Lay intended to testify tomorrow. In the midst of our preparation, particularly disturbing statements have been made by members of Congress, even today, on the eve of Mr. Lay's scheduled appearance. These inflammatory statements show tha judgments have been reached and the tenor of the hearing will be prosecutorial.

For example, on NBC's Today Show and MSNBC, Senator Peter Fitzgerald charged:

"Ken Lay obviously had to know that this was a giant pyramid scheme – a giant shell game.... They grafted a pyramid onto an old fashioned utility.... There was

CHICAGO | WASHINGTON | BALTIMORE | NEW YORK RESTON TAMPA | PHILADELPHIA | DALLAS LOS ANGELES

File 10 (Continued)

Hon. Ernest Hollings, Chairman
February 3, 2002
Page 2

blatant fraudulent activity going on for years, and in my opinion he had to have known...."

On Meet the Press today, Senator Byron Dorgan concluded:

"[T]his is almost a culture of corporate corruption...

"Clearly some things have happened here that are going to put some real people in real jeopardy and trouble."

On the same TV program, Congressman Billy Tauzin, the chair of one of the committees conducting one of the principal investigations of the Enron collapse, claimed:

"Secondly: were they really wrongdoing, and maybe somebody ought to go to the pokey for this? I think we are going to find out yes to that question."

Congressman Tauzin also charged:

"[N]ot only were there corrupt practices, not only was there a hiding of the fact that debt was being put off the balance sheets and profits were reported that didn't exist, but we've found more than that. I think we're finding what may clearly end up being securities fraud, attempts not to hedge or put debt out of the company, which many companies do, but literally fraudulent, phony attempts to do so...."

These are a few examples, from among many others. Indeed, as *The New York Times* reported today, in appearing before the subcommittee, "Mr. Lay will face a panel eager to pulverize him." As a consequence, I have instructed Mr. Lay to withdraw his prior acceptance of your invitation. He does so, but only with the greatest reluctance and regret. He also wishes to express, as do I, our sincerest apologies for any inconvenience caused by this decision, but he cannot be expected to participate in a proceeding in which conclusions have been reached before Mr. Lay has been given an opportunity to be heard.

Sincerely,

Earl Silbert

Earl J. Silbert

cc: Hon. John McCain
Hon. Byron Dorgan
Hon. Peter D. Fitzgerald

** TOTAL PAGE.05 **
** TOTAL PAGE.02 **

File 11 Memo about Enron's trading strategies in California wholesale power markets.

Reviewed for Privilege
1435
Rev'r OM Bx 4/24/003

STOEL RIVES LLP

MEMORANDUM

December 6, 2000

TO: RICHARD SANDERS

FROM: CHRISTIAN YODER AND STEPHEN HALL

RE: Traders' Strategies in the California Wholesale Power Markets/ ISO Sanctions

CONFIDENTIAL: ATTORNEY/CLIENT PRIVILEGE/ATTORNEY WORK PRODUCT

This memorandum analyzes certain trading strategies that Enron's traders are using in the California wholesale energy markets. Section A explains two popular strategies used by the traders, "inc-ing" load and relieving congestion. Section B describes and analyzes other strategies used by Enron's traders, some of which are variations on "inc-ing" load or relieving congestion. Section C discusses the sanction provisions of the California Independent System Operator ("ISO") tariff

A. The Big Picture

1. "Inc-ing" Load Into The Real Time Market

One of the most fundamental strategies used by the traders is referred to as "'inc-ing' load into the real time market." According to one trader, this is the 'oldest trick in the book' and, according to several of the traders, it is now being used by other market participants.

To understand this strategy, it is important to understand a little about the ISO's real-time market.[1] One responsibility of the ISO is to balance generation (supply) and loads (demand) on the California transmission system. During its real-time energy balancing function the ISO pays/charges market participants for increasing/decreasing their generation. The ISO pays/charges market participants under two schemes: "instructed deviations" and "uninstructed deviations." Instructed deviations occur when the ISO selects supplemental energy bids from generators offering to supply energy to the market in real time in response to ISO instructions. Market participants that increase their generation in response to instructions ("instructed deviation") from the ISO are paid the "inc" price. Market participants that increase their

[1] The "real-time" energy market is also known as the imbalance energy market. The imbalance energy market can be further subdivided into the (1) supplemental energy or instructed deviation market and (2) the ex post market or uninstructed deviation market.

File 11 (Continued)

generation without an instruction from the ISO (an "uninstructed deviation") are paid the ex post "dec" price. In real-time, the ISO issues instructions and publishes ex post prices at ten-minute intervals.

"'Inc-ing load' into the real-time market" is a strategy that enables Enron to send excess generation to the imbalance energy market as an uninstructed deviation. To participate in the imbalance energy market it is necessary to have at least 1 MW of load. The reason for this is that a generator cannot schedule energy onto the grid without having a corresponding load. The ISO requires scheduling coordinators to submit balanced schedules; i.e., generation must equal load. So, if load must equal generation, how can Enron end up with excess generation in the real-time market?

The answer is to artificially increase ("inc") the load on the schedule submitted to the ISO. Then, in real-time, Enron sends the generation it scheduled, but does not take as much load as scheduled. The ISO's meters record that Enron did not draw as much load, leaving it with an excess amount of generation. The ISO gives Enron credit for the excess generation and pays Enron the dec price multiplied by the number of excess megawatts. An example will demonstrate this Enron will submit a day-ahead schedule showing 1000 MW of generation scheduled for delivery to Enron Energy Services ("EES"). The ISO receives the schedule, which says "1000 MW of generation" and "1000 MW of load." The ISO sees that the schedule balances and, assuming there is no congestion, schedules transmission for this transaction. In real-time, Enron sends 1000 MW of generation, but Enron Energy Services only draws 500 MW. The ISO's meters show that Enron made a net contribution to the grid of 500 MW, and so the ISO pays Enron 500 times the dec price.

The traders are able to anticipate when the dec price will be favorable by comparing the ISO's forecasts with their own. When the traders believe that the ISO's forecast underestimates the expected load, they will inc load into the real time market because they know that the market will be short, causing a favorable movement in real-time ex post prices. Of course, the much-criticized strategy of California's investor-owned utilities ("IOUs") of underscheduling load in the day-ahead market has contributed to the real-time market being short. The traders have learned to build such underscheduling into their models, as well.

Two other points bear mentioning. Although Enron may have been the first to use this strategy, others have picked up on it, too. I am told this can be shown by looking at the ISO's real-time metering, which shows that an excess amount of generation, over and above Enron's contribution, is making it to the imbalance market as an uninstructed deviation. Second, Enron has performed this service for certain other customers for which it acts as scheduling coordinator. The customers using this service are companies such as Powerex and Puget Sound Energy ("PSE"), that have generation to sell, but no native California load. Because Enron has native California load through EES, it is able to submit a schedule incorporating the generation of a generator like Powerex or PSE and balance the schedule with "dummied-up" load from EES.

Interestingly, this strategy appears to benefit the reliability of the ISO's grid. It is well known the California IOUs have systematically underscheduled their load in the PX's Day-

2

File 11 (Continued)

Ahead market. By underscheduling their load into the Day-Ahead market, the IOUs have caused the ISO to have to call on energy in real time in order to keep the transmission system in balance. In other words, the transmission grid is short energy. By deliberately overscheduling load, Enron has been offsetting the ISO's real time energy deficit by supplying extra energy that the ISO needs. Also, it should be noted that in the ex post market Enron is a "price taker," meaning that they are not submitting bids or offers, but are just being paid the value of the energy that the ISO needs. If the ISO did not need the energy, the dec price would quickly drop to $0. So, the fact that Enron was getting paid for this energy shows that the ISO needed the energy to balance the transmission system and offset the IOU's underscheduling (if those parties own Firm Transmission Rights ("FTR") over the path).

2. Relieving Congestion

The second strategy used by Enron's traders is to relieve system-wide congestion in the real-time market, which congestion was created by Enron's traders in the PX's Day Ahead Market. In order to relieve transmission congestion (i.e., the energy scheduled for delivery exceeds the capacity of the transmission path), the ISO makes payments to parties that either schedule transmission in the opposite direction ("counterflow payments") or that simply reduce their generation/load schedule.

Many of the strategies used by the traders involve structuring trades so that Enron gets paid the congestion charge. Because the congestion charges have been as high as $750/MW, it can often be profitable to sell power at a loss simply to be able to collect the congestion payment.

B. Representative Trading Strategies

The strategies listed below are examples of actual strategies used by the traders, many of which utilize the two basic principles described above. In some cases, the strategies are identified by the nicknames that the traders have assigned to them. In some cases, i.e., "Fat Boy," Enron's traders have used these nicknames with traders from other companies to identify these strategies.

1. Export of California Power

   a. As a result of the price caps in the PX and ISO (currently $250), Enron has been able to take advantage of arbitrage opportunities by buying energy at the PX for export outside California. For example, yesterday (December 5, 2000), prices at Mid-C peaked at $1200, while California was capped at $250. Thus, traders could buy power at $250 and sell it for $1200.

   b. This strategy appears not to present any problems, other than a public relations risk arising from the fact that such exports may have contributed to California's declaration of a Stage 2 Emergency yesterday.

2. "Non-firm Export"

3

File 11 (Continued)

a. The goal is to get paid for sending energy in the opposite direction as the constrained path (counterflow congestion payment). Under the ISO's tariff, scheduling coordinators that schedule energy in the opposite direction of the congestion on a constrained path get paid the congestion charges, which are charged to scheduling coordinators scheduling energy in the direction of the constraint. At times, the value of the congestion payments can be greater than the value of the energy itself.

b. This strategy is accomplished by scheduling non-firm energy for delivery from SP-15 or NP-15 to a control area outside California. This energy must be scheduled three hours before delivery. After two hours, Enron gets paid the counterflow charges. A trader then cuts the non-firm power. Once the non-firm power is cut, the congestion resumes.

c. The ISO posted notice in early August prohibiting this practice. Enron's traders stopped this practice immediately following the ISO's posting.

d. The ISO objected to the fact that the generators were cutting the non-firm energy. The ISO would not object to this transaction if the energy was eventually exported.

Apparently, the ISO has heavily documented Enron's use of this strategy. Therefore, this strategy is the more likely than most to receive attention from the ISO.

2. "Death Star"

a. This strategy earns money by scheduling transmission in the opposite direction of congestion; i.e., schedule transmission north in the summertime and south in the winter, and then collecting the congestion payments. No energy, however, is actually put onto the grid or taken off.

b. For example, Enron would first import non-firm energy at Lake Mead for export to the California-Oregon border ("COB"). Because the energy is traveling in the opposite direction of a constrained line, Enron gets paid for the counterflow. Enron also avoids paying ancillary service charges for this export because the energy is non-firm, and the ISO tariff does not require the purchase of ancillary services for non-firm energy.

c. Second, Enron buys transmission from COB to Lake Mead at tariff rates to serve the import. The transmission line from COB to Lake Mead is outside of the ISO's control area, so the ISO is unaware that the same energy being exported from Lake Mead is simultaneously being imported into Lake Mead. Similarly, because the COB to Lake Mead line is outside the ISO's control area, Enron is not subject to payment of congestion charges because transmission charges for the COB to Lake Mead line are assessed based on imbedded costs.

4

File 11 (Continued)

d. The ISO probably cannot readily detect this practice because the ISO only sees what is happening inside its control area, so it only sees half of the picture.

e. The net effect of these transactions is that Enron gets paid for moving energy to relieve congestion without actually moving any energy or relieving any congestion.

3. "Load Shift"

a. This strategy is applied to the Day-Ahead and the real-time markets.

b. Enron shifts load from a congested zone to a less congested zone, thereby earning payments for reducing congestion, i.e., not using our FTRs on a constrained path.

c. This strategy requires that Enron have FTRs connecting the two zones.

d. A trader will overschedule load in one zone, i.e., SP-15, and underschedule load in another zone, i.e., NP-15.

Such scheduling will often raise the congestion price in the zone where load was overscheduled.

The trader will then "shift" the overscheduled "load" to the other zone, and get paid for the unused FTRs. The ISO pays the congestion charge (if there is one) to market participants that do not use their FTRs. The effect of this action is to create the appearance of congestion through the deliberate overstatement of loads, which causes the ISO to charge congestion charges to supply scheduled for delivery in the congested zone. Then, by reverting back to its true load in the respective zones, Enron is deemed to have relieved congestion, and gets paid by the ISO for so doing.

e. One concern here is that by knowingly increasing the congestion costs, Enron is effectively increasing the costs to all market participants in the real time market.

f. Following this strategy has produced profits of approximately $30 million for FY 2000.

4. "Get Shorty"

a. Under this strategy, Enron sells ancillary services in the Day-ahead market.

b. Then, the next day, in the real-time market, a trader "zeroes out" the ancillary services, i.e., cancels the commitment and buys ancillary services in the real-time market to cover its position.

5

File 11 (Continued)

c. The profit is made by shorting the ancillary services, i.e., sell high and buy back at a lower price.

d. One concern here is that the traders are applying this strategy without having the ancillary services on standby. The traders are careful, however, to be sure to buy services right at 9:00 a.m. so that Enron is not actually called upon to provide ancillary services. However, once, by accident, a trader inadvertently failed to cover, and the ISO called on those ancillary services.

e. This strategy might be characterized as "paper trading," because the seller does not actually have the ancillary services to sell. FERC recently denied Morgan Stanley's request to paper trade on the New York ISO.

The ISO tariff does provide for situations where a scheduling coordinator sells ancillary services in the day ahead market, and then reduces them in the day-of market. Under these circumstances, the tariff simply requires that the scheduling coordinator replace the capacity in the hour-ahead market. ISO Tariff, SBP 5.3, *Buy Back of Ancillary Services.*

f. The ISO tariff requires that schedules and bids for ancillary services identify the specific generating unit or system unit, or in the case of external imports, the selling entity. As a consequence, in order to short the ancillary services it is necessary to submit false information that purports to identify the source of the ancillary services.

5. "Wheel Out"

a. This strategy is used when the interties are set to zero, i.e., completely constrained.

b. First, knowing that the intertie is completely constrained, Enron schedules a transmission flow through the system. By so doing, Enron earns the congestion charge. Second, because the line's capacity is set to "0," the traders know that any power scheduled to go through the inter-tie will, in fact be cut. Therefore, Enron earns the congestion counterflow payment without having to actually send energy through the intertie.

c. As a rule, the traders have learned that money can be made through congestion charges when a transmission line is out of service because the ISO will never schedule an energy delivery because the intertie is constrained.

6. "Fat Boy"

a. This strategy is described above in section A (1).

7. "Ricochet"

6

File 11 (Continued)

a. Enron buys energy from the PX in the Day Of market, and schedules it for export. The energy is sent out of California to another party, which charges a small fee per MW, and then Enron buys it back to sell the energy to the ISO real-time market.

b. The effect of this strategy on market prices and supply is complex. First, it is clear that Enron's intent under this strategy is solely to arbitrage the spread between the PX and the ISO, and not to serve load or meet contractual obligations. Second, Ricochet may increase the Market Clearing Price by increasing the demand for energy. (Increasing the MCP does not directly benefit Enron because it is *buying* energy from the PX, but it certainly affects other buyers, who must pay the same, higher price.) Third, Ricochet appears to have a neutral effect on supply, because it is returning the exported energy as an import. Fourth, the parties that pay Enron for supplying energy to the real time ex post market are the parties that underscheduled, or underestimated their load, i.e., the IOUs.

8. Selling Non-firm Energy as Firm Energy

a. The traders commonly sell non-firm energy to the PX as "firm." "Firm energy," in this context, means that the energy includes ancillary services. The result is that the ISO pays EPMI for ancillary services that Enron claims it is providing, but does not in fact provide.

b. The traders claim that "everybody does this," especially for imports from the Pacific Northwest into California.

c. At least one complaint was filed with the ISO regarding Enron's practice of doing this. Apparently, Arizona Public Service sold non-firm energy to Enron, which turned around and sold the energy to the ISO as firm. APS cut the energy flow, and then called the ISO and told the ISO what Enron had done.

9. Scheduling Energy To Collect the Congestion Charge II

a. In order to collect the congestion charges, the traders may schedule a counterflow even if they do not have any excess generation. In real time, the ISO will see that Enron did deliver the energy it promised, so it will charge Enron the inc price for each MW Enron was short. The ISO, however, still pays Enron the congestion charge. Obviously a loophole, which the ISO could close by simply failing to pay congestion charges to entities that failed to deliver the energy.

b. This strategy is profitable whenever the congestion charge is sufficiently greater than the price cap. In other words, since the ex post is capped at $250, whenever the congestion charge is greater than $250 it is profitable to schedule counterflows, collect the congestion charge, pay the ex post, and keep the difference.

C. **ISO Tariff**

7

File 11 (Continued)

The ISO tariff prohibits "gaming," which it defines as follows:

> "Gaming," or taking unfair advantage of the rules and procedures set forth in the PX or ISO Tariffs, Protocols or Activity Rules, or of transmission constraints in period in which exist substantial Congestion, to the detriment of the efficiency of, and of consumers in, the ISO Markets. "Gaming" may also include taking undue advantage of other conditions that may affect the availability of transmission and generation capacity, such as loop flow, facility outages, level of hydropower output or seasonal limits on energy imports from out-of-state, or actions or behaviors that may otherwise render the system and the ISO Markets vulnerable to price manipulation to the detriment of their efficiency." ISO Market Monitoring and Information Protocol ("MMIP"), Section 2.1.3.

The ISO tariff also prohibits "anomalous market behavior," which includes "unusual trades or transactions"; "pricing and bidding patterns that are inconsistent with prevailing supply and demand conditions"; and "unusual activity or circumstances relating to imports from or exports to other markets or exchanges." MMIP, Section 2.1.1 et seq.

Should it discover such activities, the ISO tariff provides that the ISO may take the following action:

1. Publicize such activities or behavior and its recommendations thereof, "*in whatever medium it believes most appropriate.*" MMIP, Section 2.3.2 (emphasis added).

2. The Market Surveillance Unit may recommend actions, including fines and suspensions, against specific entities in order to deter such activities or behavior. MMIP, Section 2.3.2.

3. With respect to allegations of gaming, the ISO may order ADR procedures to determine if a particular practice is better characterized as improper gaming or "legitimate aggressive competition." MMIP, Section 2.3.3.

4. In cases of "serious abuse requiring expeditious investigation or action" the Market Surveillance Unit shall refer a matter to the appropriate regulatory or antitrust enforcement agency. MMIP, Section 3.3.4.

5. Any Market Participant or interested entity may file a complaint with the Market Surveillance Unit. Following such complaint, the Market Surveillance Unit may "carry out any investigation that it considers appropriate as to the concern raised." MMIP, Section 3.3.5.

6. The ISO Governing Board may impose "such sanctions or penalties as it believes necessary and as are permitted under the ISO Tariff and related protocols approved by FERC; or it may refer the matter to such regulatory or antitrust agency as it sees fit to recommend the imposition of sanctions and penalties." MMIP, Section 7.3.

8

References

Ackman, Dan. 2002. "No Sweat for Skilling." Forbes.com (February 27).

Ahrens, Frank. 2002. "Enron Expects Asset Write-Off of $14 Billion." *Washington Post* (April 23).

"Azurix: The Roller-Coaster Years." 2002. *Platts Global Water Report* (January 25).

Banjeree, Nela. 2002. "At Enron, Lavish Excess Often Came before Success." *New York Times* (February 2).

"Bankruptcy Judge Approves $1,110 for Each Laid-Off Enron Worker." 2002. *Houston Chronicle* (March 5).

Barboza, David, and Barnaby Feder. 2002. "Enron's Swap with Qwest Questioned." *New York Times* (March 29).

Barboza, David, and Kurt Eichenwald. 2002. "Lay's Son, Sister Profited from Dealings with Enron." *New York Times* (February 1).

Barnes, Julian, Megan Barnett, and Christopher Schmidt. 2002. "How a Titan Came Undone." *U.S. News & World Report* (March 18). www.usnews.com/usnews/biztech/articles/020318/18enron.htm.

Baxter, J. Clifford. 2002. Suicide note found on January 25.

Behr, Peter. 2001. "Enron Discloses SEC Inquiry." *Washington Post* (October 23), page E03.

Behr, Peter. 2001. "Enron Says Profit Was Overstated." *Washington Post* (October 23).

Behr, Peter. 2002. "How Chewco Brought Down an Empire." *Washington Post* (February 4).

Behr, Peter, and April Witt. 2002. "Ex-Enron Executive Related a Dispute." *Washington Post* (March 18). www.washingtonpost.com/wp-dyn/articles/A47396-2002Mar18.html.

Behr, Peter, and Dan Eggen. 2002. "Enron Is Target of Criminal Probe." *Washington Post* (January 10).

Behr, Peter, and Robert O'Harrow Jr. 2002. "$270 Million Man Stays in the Background." *Washington Post* (February 6), page A01.

Berthelsen, Christian, and Scott Winokur. 2001. "Chairman Pitches His Plan to Prominent Californians." *San Francisco Chronicle* (May 26).

Bierman, Harold, Jr. 2002. "The Enron Collapse." Unpublished manuscript (May).

Bivins, Ralph. 2001. "Ripples from Enron Hit Downtown." *Houston Chronicle* (December 5).

Brenner, Marie. 2002. "The Enron Wars." *Vanity Fair* Issue No. 500 (April).

"Bush and Enron's Collapse." 2002. *The Economist* (January 11). www.economist.com/agenda/displayStory.cfm?story_id=938154.

"CalPERS and Enron: The Losses, the Relationship, and the Future." CalPERS web site: www.calpers.ca.gov/whatshap/hottopic/enron.htm.

Ceconi, Margaret. 2001. E-mail to Kenneth Lay (August 29).

Chatterjee, Sajan, and Batten Fellow. 2002. "Enron's Strategy: The Good, Bad, and the Ugly; What Can We Learn?" Unpublished manuscript (January).

"Could Have Been Much More." 2001. *The Desk* (November 30).

"Dynegy Confirms Discussions with Enron." 2001. Dynegy Inc. corporate press release (November 8).

"Dynegy and Enron Announce Merger Agreement." 2001. Dynegy Inc. corporate press release (November 9).

"Dynegy Terminates Merger with Enron." 2001. Dynegy Inc. corporate press release (November 28).

Enron 1998 Annual Report. 1999.

Enron 1999 Annual Report. 2000.

Enron 2000 Annual Report. 2001.

"Enron and Enron Oil & Gas Announce Share Exchange Agreement, Creating Independent EOG." 1999. Enron corporate press release (July 20).

"Enron Announces J-Block Settlement." 1997. Enron corporate press release (June 2).

"Enron Announces Promotion of Jeff Skilling to CEO, Ken Lay Remains as Chairman of the Board." 2001. Enron corporate press release (December 13).

"Enron Announces Skilling Resignation; Lay Assumes President and CEO Duties." 2001. Enron corporate press release (August 14).

"The Enron Bankruptcy." 2002. www.cspan.org.

"Enron Board of Directors." 2002. *Guardian Unlimited* (March 21 download).

"Enron Capital & Trade Resources to Purchase New Jersey Power Plants." 1998. Enron corporate press release (October 30).

"Enron India, Mauritius Subsidiaries File for Bankruptcy." 2002. Platts.com (March 21).

"Enron Makes a Bold Move into California Electricity Market." 1997. Enron corporate press release (October 23).

"Enron Named Most Innovative Company for Sixth Year." 2001. Enron corporate press release (February 6).

"Enron Provides Additional Information about Related Party and Off-Balance Sheet Transactions; Company to Restate Earnings for 1997–2001." 2001. Enron corporate press release (November 8).

"Enron Reports Record First Quarter Recurring Earnings of $0.47 per Diluted Share; Increases Earnings Expectations for 2001." 2001. Enron corporate press release (April 17).

"Enron Scandal Brings Overdue Scrutiny of Analysts." 2002. *USA Today* (March 24).

"Enron's J Clifford Baxter: A Profile." 2002. BBC News. (January 27). www.bbc.co.uk.

"Enron: Skilling Blames Others." 2001. http://money.cnn.com (February 26).

"Enron's Rebecca Mark: 'You Have to Be Pushy and Aggressive.'" 1997. *Business Week* (February 24).

"Enron Vice Chairman Cliff Baxter Resigns." 2001. Enron corporate press release (May 2).

Fink, Roland. 2002. "Beyond Enron." *CFO Magazine* (February).

Frey, Jennifer. 2002. "Low-Profile Partnership Head Stayed on Job Until Judge's Order." *Washington Post* (February 7), p. A15.

Fusaro, Peter. 2000. *Energy Derivatives: Trading Emerging Markets.* New York: Energy Publishing Enterprises.

Fusaro, Peter. 2001. "California Energy Crisis Report." New York: Global Change Associates (March).

Fusaro, Peter. 2001. *Enron 2001: An Inside View.* New York: Global Change Associates (July).

Gruley, Bryan, and Rebecca Smith. 2002. "Anatomy of a Fall: Keys to Success Left Kenneth Lay Open to Disaster." *Wall Street Journal* (April 26).

Hanson, Eric. 2002. "Attorney General Orders Release of ex-Enron Executive's Suicide Note." *Houston Chronicle* (April 11, 5:59 P.M.). www.chron.com/cs/CDA/story.hts/special/enron/1361816.

"Indian State Spurred by Enron Reopens Power Deals." 2001. Reuters Newswire (May 22).

Ivanovich, David. 2002. "Local Feds, Ashcroft Recused from Inquiry." *Houston Chronicle* (January 11).

Jameson, Rob. 2001. "Enron's Off-Balance Machine." ERisk.com (December).

Johnson, Carrie. 2002. "Enron Case Shapes Up as Tough Legal Fight." *Washington Post* (February 18).

Kaplan, David, and L. M. Sixel. 2001. "Enron Lays Off 4,000." *Houston Chronicle* (December 4).

Ketcham, Christopher. 2002. "Enron's Human Toll." Salon.com (January 23).

Krandell, Kathryn. 2002. "Taking Fifth before Congress Hasn't Always Been a Public Affair." *Wall Street Journal* (February 13).

Krantz, Matt. 2002. "Trouble Brewing in Enron's Interlinking Partnerships." *USA Today* (January 21).

Lay, Kenneth. 2001. E-mail to employees dated October 2.

"Lay Resigns as Chairman and CEO of Enron, Remains on Board of Directors." 2002. Enron press release (January 23).

LeBoutillier, John. 2002. "From Harvard to Enron." *New York Daily News* (January 10).

"Letter from Lay's Attorney to Committee Chair." 2002. www.cnn.com (February 3).

Levitt, Arthur, Jr. 2002. "What's Bred in the Bone." *Bloomberg Personal Finance* (April).

Lynch, Kevin, Michael Hanrahan, and David Wright. 2002. "Enron: Exclusive *Enquirer* Investigation." *National Enquirer* (February 25).

"Man on the Hot Seat." 2002. *U.S. News & World Report* (January 28).

Mason, Julie. 2001. "Andersen Fires Enron Auditor." *Houston Chronicle* (January 16).

Mason, Julie. 2002. "Congressmen Cry Foul in Enron's Self-Investigation." *Houston Chronicle* (February 1). www.chron.com/cs/CDA/story.hts/special/enron/1237367.

Mason, Julie. 2002. "Employee Note Warned Lay." *Houston Chronicle* (January 15).

McLean, Bethany. 2001. "Is Enron Overpriced?" *Fortune* (March 5).

McLean, Bethany. 2001. "Why Enron Went Bust." *Fortune* (December 24).

Miller, Ross M. 2002. *Paving Wall Street: Experimental Economics and the Quest for the Perfect Market.* New York: John Wiley & Sons.

Moody's Special Comment. 2001. "The Unintended Consequences of Rating Triggers." (December 7).

"One Big Client, One Big Hassle." 2002. Special Report. *Business Week* (January 28).

"The Players." 2002. *Houston Chronicle* (January 24, 2:52 P.M.). www.chron.com/cs/CDA/story.hts/special/enron/1127106.

Powers, William C., Jr., Raymond S. Troubh, and Herbert S. Winokur Jr. 2002. *Report of Investigation by the Special Investigation Committee of the Board of Directors of Enron Corp.* (February 1).

Puscas, Darren. 2002. "A Guide to the Enron Collapse." *Corporate Profiles* (Canadian Centre for Policy Alternatives) (March).

Roberts, Johnny, and Evan Thomas. 2002. "Enron's Dirty Laundry." *Newsweek* (March 11).

Robinson, Edward. 2002. "The NewPower Debacle." *Bloomberg Markets* (January).

Romano, Lois, and Paul Duggan. 2002. " 'Low-Profile Guy' Was Wizard Behind Enron's Complex Books." *Washington Post* (February 7), p. A15.

Schmitt, Christopher, Megan Barrett, Julian Baines, and Kit Roane. 2002. *U.S. News & World Report* (January 28).

Schwartz, John. 2002. "Darth Vader. Machiavelli. Skilling Set Intense Pace." *New York Times* (January 7).

Scotti, Ciro. 2002. "How to Make the Enron Gang Pay." *Business Week* (February 21).

"Seeds of Scandal." 2002. *U.S. News & World Report* (March 18).

"Selling High." 2002. *Washington Post* (January 27), p. A10.

Shook, Barbara. 2001. "Future Enron Seen as Mere Shadow." *Oil Daily* (December 5).

Smith, Rebecca. 2002. "New Power Saga Shows How Enron Tapped IPO Boom to Boost Results." *Wall Street Journal* (March 26).

Smithson, Charles. 1996. *Managing Financial Risk 1996 Yearbook.* New York: Canadian Imperial Bank of Commerce.

Smithson, Charles. 1997. *Managing Financial Risk 1997 Yearbook.* New York: Canadian Imperial Bank of Commerce.

Smithson, Charles. 1998. *Managing Financial Risk 1998 Yearbook.* New York: Canadian Imperial Bank of Commerce.

Smithson, Charles. 1999. *Managing Financial Risk 1999 Yearbook.* New York: Canadian Imperial Bank of Commerce.

Stark, Betsy. 2002. "Enron Caution Prompts Analyst Firing." abcNEWS.com (March 26).

Steffy, Loren. 2002. "Andrew Fastow: Mystery CFO." *Bloomberg Markets* (January).

Stewart, James B. 1991. *Den of Thieves.* New York: Simon & Schuster.

Swartz, Mimi. 2002. "Houston Postcard: An Enron Yard Sale." *New Yorker* (May 8).

"Taking Stock." 2002. *Washington Post* (February 4), p. A04.

"These Boots Are Made for Walking." 2002. *GARP Risk Review* (March/April).

"Timeline: Enron." 2002. *Guardian Unlimited* (February 4). http://guardian.co.uk/enron/story/0,11337.638640.00 html.

"Timeline of Enron's Collapse." 2002. *Washington Post* (February 25). http://washingtonpost.com/wp-dyn/articles/A25624-2001Jan10.html.

Tran, Mark. 2002. "Enron Sting Used Fake Command Center." *Guardian* (February 21).

Tufano, Peter, and Sanjay Bhatnagar. 1994. "Enron Gas Services." Harvard Business School Case Study 9-294-076.

Useem, Michael. 2002. "Enron's Kenneth Lay: The Last Road Not Taken." *Knowledge @ Wharton* online biweekly newsletter (April 10–23). http://knowledge.wharton.upenn.edu/articles.cfm?catid=2&articleid=541.

Wallstin, Brian. 2002. "Living in a House of Cards." *Houston Press* (March 28).

Watkins, Sherron. 2001. Letter to Ken Lay (August).

Wee, Heesun. 2002. "Kinder Morgan's Brunch with Enronitis." *Business Week* (March 11).

Weiss, Stephen. 2001. "The Fall of a Giant: Enron's Campaign Contribution and Lobbying." www.opensecrets.org (November 9).

Welch, Jack, with John A. Byrne. 2001. *Jack: Straight from the Gut*. New York: Warner Books.

White, Ben. 2002. "House Panel Wants Wall Street Enron Data." *Washington Post* (March 7).

Whitlock, Craig, and Peter Behr. 2002. "CEO Pushed Hard for Transformation of Firm." *Washington Post* (February 15).

Zellner, Wendy. 2002. "Jeffrey Skilling: Enron's Missing Man." *Business Week* (February 11).

Zellner, Wendy, and Stephanie Anderson Forest. 2001. "The Fall of Enron." *Business Week* (December 17).

About the Authors

Peter C. Fusaro is founder and President of Global Change Associates, an energy consulting firm. Over the past 13 years, he has written extensively about the energy industry, energy risk management, and Enron. His research on Enron, its business operations, and its corporate culture was extensive prior to the firm's bankruptcy and is now regularly referenced by those investigating the firm's dramatic collapse. He is the author of *Energy Derivatives: Trading Emerging Markets*, *Energy Risk Management*, and *Energy Convergence: The Beginning of the Multi-Commodity Market*.

Fusaro has worked for 27 years in the international energy business and is a frequent speaker at energy conferences throughout the world. He is adviser to the U.S. Department of Energy and New York Chapter President of the International Association of Energy Economics. He received a B.A. from Carnegie-Mellon University and an M.A. in international relations from Tufts University.

Ross M. Miller is founder and President of Miller Risk Advisors. After several years of teaching finance and economics at the University of Houston, California Institute of Technology, and Boston University, he established the quantitative finance research group at General Electric and was Senior Vice President and Director of Research at an international investment bank. He is the author of *Paving Wall Street: Experimental Economics and the Quest for the Perfect Market* and *Computer-Aided Financial Analysis.*

Miller is regarded as a pioneer in experimental economics and has consulted for the Federal Trade Commission and the U.S. State Department. He is also well known for his research on intelligent electronic market systems, often referred to simply as "smart markets." He received a B.S. in mathematics from the California Institute of Technology and a Ph.D. in economics from Harvard University. He lives in Niskayuna, New York, with his wife and two children.

Index

INDEX

Index

Index